Pr to

It is great.

Sincerely
Jim Lake
Grandview Life.

RUSH

RUSH

Get set for extreme sales, starting today!

Robert J. Smith

iUniverse, Inc.
New York   Bloomington

The information, ideas, and suggestions in this book are not intended to render professional advice. Before following any suggestions contained in this book, you should consult your personal accountant or other financial advisor. Neither the author nor the publisher shall be liable or responsible for any loss or damage allegedly arising as a consequence of your use or application of any information or suggestions in this book.

iUniverse books may be ordered through booksellers or by contacting:

iUniverse
1663 Liberty Drive
Bloomington, IN 47403
www.iuniverse.com
1-800-Authors (1-800-288-4677)

Because of the dynamic nature of the Internet, any Web addresses or links contained in this book may have changed since publication and may no longer be valid. The views expressed in this work are solely those of the author and do not necessarily reflect the views of the publisher, and the publisher hereby disclaims any responsibility for them.

ISBN: 978-1-4401-7541-1 (sc)
ISBN: 978-1-4401-7540-4 (ebook)
ISBN: 978-1-4401-7539-8 (hc)

Library of Congress Control Number: 2009937342

Printed in the United States of America

iUniverse rev. date: 12/02/2009

To the loves of my life,
Jodi, Taylor, Danielle, Madison.

To my parents, to whom I owe everything,
Bob, Peggy.

To my best friend, Greg.

Contents

Acknowledgments

First, I would like to sincerely thank Steve Holstein for all of your hard work, direction, and commitment to RUSH. Your gift of writing brought life to RUSH. Thank you for your professionalism and insight. I could not have completed this project without you.

To Lorna Dyer, my office manager, business partner, and friend: I cannot tell you how much I appreciate everything you do. Your wisdom and advice are irreplaceable.

Katy Hartley, thank you for managing the project of writing, advertising, and marketing *RUSH*. Your expertise and work ethic are invaluable to me.

Introduction

I'm a salesman and proud of it.

In fact, I've been a salesman literally *every day* for the past twenty-five years. I live the same life as you—the highs and the lows. I have failed, have been broke, and have had my share of ruts.

But along the way, I figured "it" out. I have turned around an average sales career to be among the top 10 percent of salespeople in the financial services industry. It's not by accident that my road to success is very well traveled. For generations, it has been traveled by salespeople who have gone on to become legends within their respective industries.

Unfortunately, that road is completely hidden to many. Salespeople today have lost their way and are desperate for guidance and *meaningful* training. Many feel they have no choice but to give up on their dreams of financial security. Others are growing weary of the status quo—tired of whiners and mediocrity within their work environment. They're not sure which way to turn.

If this resonates with you, you are reading the right book. If you're feeling good about your sales capabilities, but trying to be just that much better, you too are reading the right book. If you're ready to tear down your sales game for the ultimate purpose of rebuilding and becoming a sales legend in your own time—read on.

RUSH will take you down the road that has been taken for generations by sales greats who consistently outproduce 90 percent of their peers.

You will be amazed by the simplicity of it all. However, it is hard work, and it will likely change your perspective on how to succeed. I will make you uncomfortable, challenge you, and quite possibly make you very upset. I'm not trying to win a popularity contest or be your friend. I don't care about what consultants or management says. Don't expect any new strategies, long-held secrets, or bleeding-edge fads. *RUSH* is simply about what works and what is used *every day* by those who are the very best.

My proof is the accomplishments of our legends. They have made their strategies readily available to everyone. We just need to be willing to read and emulate them.

Many will not. But a few will.

I would like to point out that I began writing *RUSH* in December of 2007 and finished in early 2009. My, how things changed during that time, as the global economy headed into some of the worst economic challenges in decades.

We sales professionals take the brunt of such downturns, as we try to move products and services when no one seems to be buying. During this time, there wasn't a day that went by that I didn't hear or read about consultants and management teams coming up with *reactive* strategies or efforts to respond to the economy by going *back to basics*.

They just don't get it. They never do.

If you are *reacting* to a market, whether it's going up or down, you are already too late. And *back to basics*? Are you kidding me? The basics of focusing on referrals and client communication should never have been left in the first place. Top salespeople are ALL about the basics and being *proactive*.

Always have been. Always will be.

So, while 90 percent of salespeople experienced financial pain, shock, depression, and desperation during this time, 10 percent were likely having some of the best years of their careers. Business pouring in. New clients calling every day.

I doubled my best year in 2008.

How does that happen? Luck? Secret strategies?

No. Simply emulating what sales legends have been doing for generations.

My research and this book will prove it to you. There is nothing new, creative, or magical about what we do day in and day out. A down market only confirms *RUSH* and the activities of the greats. The legends have handed down the absolute truths of how to be successful in any market. *RUSH* embodies their success in performing on a high level, *every day*. Every tool, strategy, and mind-set described can be put into place *today*.

I will show you exactly what it's like to practice the fundamentals of sales--one day at a time. The key is to focus on performing extreme activities *every day* in order to satisfy our craving for a RUSH. I know that anyone who aspires to be a sales leader seeks and craves their daily adrenaline RUSH. This RUSH is available to you and me every day by simply doing the things that challenge us.

Many will not. But a few will.

Are you ready for change? Do you think you have what it takes? Are you tired of being told what to do by management and consultants? Do you want to learn from those who have proven themselves year in and year out? I hope so.

If you are ready for hard-core, old-school, proven strategies delivered by someone who can relate to every emotion, challenge, excuse, failure, and success known to our industry, *RUSH* will change your career and quite possibly your life.

I hope *RUSH* becomes a resource to help you keep on track and confirm what *must* be done *every day*.

Are you ready and willing to make some radical changes? Then, I'll see you in Chapter 1.

Bob

A Salesperson's Profile, Who We Are, What Drives Us

Chapter 1: Wired

Sprinter or marathon runner: which one are you?

Both are enviable athletes. It's just that one has the makings for a great sales career and the other, well, as they say, "need not apply."

As sales professionals, we are a very special but, unfortunately, often misunderstood breed. We're the round pegs that companies keep trying to push through very square policies and procedures.

They want to plan, strategize, and forecast. We want to call, meet, and sell. They like a predictable future. We want to make something happen. NOW!

That's the way we're wired. We're sprinters. We're doers. We're all about putting everything we've got—our skills, our emotions, our determination, and our ego—into the thrill, elation, and absolute RUSH that we get from a win.

But unlike the planners, strategizers, and forecasters to whom we often report, we have an insatiable need to satisfy our craving for that euphoric feeling of victory every day. Why even think about the next race until we have today won and behind us?

Whether you like it or not, you and I are wired to be in the moment and live for the RUSH. It's what sets us apart. It's why we do what we do for a living. We sell.

I have been in the financial services industry for twenty-five years. I have tried just about every marketing and sales concept known to my industry. I have had tremendous highs and horrific lows. I have been on incredible runs and have had my share of ruts. I have made more money than most people and have been so broke I couldn't pay my bills. Phones get slammed. People get ugly. No one returns calls. Others carry on, telling me their life story.

You too?

This book was originally intended for my eyes only. It started out as an introspective look into my own career. I wanted to clean house! I read a lot. Listened a lot. I've picked up a lot of information over the years. What really works? What doesn't? I wasn't really sure. As creatures of habit, if something works once, we tend to hold onto that practice forever. You just never know when it might work again. I wanted to identify, focus on, and continually repeat the actions, feelings, and techniques that have consistently contributed to my success.

And so, I began to write.

As I began to write and implement my core beliefs, I found myself being in the "zone" more often at work. The zone? If you're an athlete, you may understand. But let me try to explain.

Being in the zone is a state of mind and physical experience where everything you do is exceptional and natural. You cannot predict when or why it happens, but you know you are there. It is the most euphoric feeling. Everything you know and all of your physical gifts come together, completely focused on the moment.

Professional athlete or professional salesperson. On the field or on the phone. The emotional reward that comes from being in the zone—of focusing on the moment, of excelling beyond expectations—is what sales and *RUSH* are all about.

My career changed the day I decided to focus on the here and now. My day consists of doing the key activities that will lead to big results today. The adrenaline RUSH I get from big results drives me to the next big task. A day of results and feeling the RUSH is my idea of being in the zone.

My goal is to teach you how to reorganize your thoughts and find your RUSH. So, let me pose a question.

If we agree that we are all looking for the adrenaline RUSH that comes from accomplishing a big task, making a hard call, or conducting a great meeting, then why do we spend so much time using tools and strategies that take us away from the very thing that drives us? Today's books, seminars, technology, and other tools overlook the fundamental concept that sales is emotional. We are energized by emotion. Anything that takes away from our ability to feel that emotion—to have that RUSH—is taking away from the level of success we will have in our day and ultimately in our career.

Don't get me wrong. Long-term planning is important. But those of us who are out there pounding the pavement, slamming the phones, and pushing the contracts can't do it at the expense of building a plan for what needs to be done today. If you continue building and executing your daily plan—one day after the other—I will guarantee you amazing results. You will look back after one year and will know with confidence how you did it—one day at a time.

And oh, the simplicity of it all! Can you control a day? Yes. Can you control a year? No. Do you know what you should be doing now? Yes. Do you know what you will be doing in the future? No. If your days are anything like mine, everything can change with just one phone call. You may receive a referral today that can change your entire year. Things happen; change is inevitable.

This entire book is built on the foundation of maximizing your day—finding your RUSH and making the sale. You may find the strategies to be old school: not cutting edge or fashionable; nothing sexy or particularly easy.

But what you will find is they work. Why?

I have learned everything I know from the legends of my industry. The core fundamentals of successful selling have never changed. What worked back in the day, still works today. Although we live in a fast-paced, instant-gratification society, the fundamentals still apply.

Sure, technology is an important tool in our arsenal, but we need to keep it in perspective and keep it in its place. Indeed, technology helps make a sale, but it does NOT make the salesperson. It may change how we do business, but it doesn't change the fundamentals. Your products and services can change, but the fundamentals of selling them will not. Nothing can take the place of you doing the "heavy lifting."

Truly successful sales professionals have focused, and always will focus, on the basics. Many of you who are new to the business of sales may have never studied the basics. If you choose to continue reading, I guarantee you will own them. For those of you who are in a rut, odds are you have strayed from the fundamentals. And finally, for those of you who are already successful, but not content, please read on.

What you all will find is that *RUSH* has been written to provide you with strategies that can be implemented immediately. Each chapter focuses on one specific topic with a theme of how, when, and why each tool can dramatically change your daily activities.

We will begin by eavesdropping in on the greatest moment of my career. This moment will provide you with the opportunity to see all of the tools discussed throughout this book working together in absolute harmony.

Next, we will home in on the central message of *RUSH* by enforcing the value of being focused on the day. TODAY! What's going to happen from the moment we take our cell phone off of the charger until we shut down our laptop? If we don't attack today like it is our last … it may well be.

Once you fully appreciate and understand the significance behind that mind-set, we will begin to analyze our need for the adrenaline RUSH. We will create an understanding of this natural, intense feeling of euphoria—why we're hooked on it, and how to control it, use it, and channel it for achieving extreme levels of profitability.

Then we will look at what it means to be bold. Our success absolutely depends on our ability to make things happen—every day. Put information in front of people. Move the decision process along. Confront naysayers. Get a decision. GO! Get it done. NOW! It's essential. So much so, that I often tell people, "Go bold, or go home."

Often, it's not the big things that trip us up or take us away from our game. It's the little distractions that seep into our day-to-day activities. We hear about "new" ways of doing things to shortcut the sales process. Sorry. But as you will learn, these shortcuts are simply distractions that waste your time and bring your sales efforts to a dead stop.

At this point in the book, we will stop and assess where you are along the path toward achieving your professional dreams. We will begin to build a new model and mind-set that will dramatically change how you tackle your day moving forward. As we move on, many of you will become uncomfortable with how you have been conducting yourself up to this point in your career. That is a good thing. Just be open-minded to a different approach to a successful career.

"Seek Out Your Industry Legends" is one of the most important chapters you will read. I cannot stress enough how important it will be for you to research the process utilized by the truly successful sales professionals of your industry. I recognize that my industry will be different from yours. But I can, with confidence, state that the fundamentals of sales will apply.

As we move forward, it will be important to pause for a reality check. It is a fact that one must eat while hunting big game. Often, we salespeople become so consumed by the RUSH and our quest for the "big deal" that we ignore writing smaller accounts to keep the lights on. And unfortunately … the lights do get turned off. I want to be sure that doesn't happen to you.

"Go Big" is my favorite chapter. It represents the most effective strategy I have ever implemented in my career. Make one big call, or attend one big meeting, or make one big contact. *Every day.* It feeds that fundamental need to feel the RUSH. It also feeds that need for a daily challenge. It sounds easy. It's not. But the effort is worth it!

By staying focused on what works, you will continually move forward with bold actions that help create "the Big Mo." It's the very thing that turns great athletes into superstars. It works for sales professionals too. Creating and sustaining momentum will become a key piece of our discussion. Momentum is all about capitalizing on one positive moment and parlaying it into the next—and making that happen throughout the day. And then, from day to day and week to week. It is possible! It does work!

Quite frankly, however, nothing in this book is going to be of help if you are out there making a lot of cold calls. Sorry to be so blunt. At the end of the day, it is all about referrals. Next to closing a sale, asking for referrals is the most important thing you can possibly do. It's so important that I start the process long before I close the sale. I'll show you how.

As we begin to come to a conclusion, I will bring all of our lessons together to show you how it looks and feels to have a day that will change your career. *I* will show you how to get there. *You* will need to commit to the strategy and implement it one day at a time.

The last chapter will take a look at how to perform in a tough economic market. As I write this book, we are all going through one of the toughest economic times of our generation. We have a choice to let it defeat us or inspire us. We will work together through this chapter to discover the opportunities available to us when others just want to whine. I sincerely believe that tough times represent great opportunities for those of us who are bold and disciplined.

What is written in this book has made my career what it is—putting me in the top 10 percent of my industry. I hope that *RUSH* can provide you the inspiration and confidence to improve your sales skills. I look forward to our journey together and hope you get as excited while reading this book as I did while writing it.

Let's begin.

Chapter 1: Questions to Consider

- Do you put everything you have into the moment to make something happen now?
- Do you have an insatiable need to satisfy your craving for the adrenaline RUSH every day?
- Have you ever felt being in the "zone," with everything you know and all your physical gifts coming together, completely focused on the moment?
- Have you ever considered focusing on the day, the here and now?
- Do you find your adrenaline RUSH by making a big call, conducting a big meeting, or accomplishing a big task?
- Are you tired of hearing from consultants and management about how to be an extreme sales professional?
- Are you interested in learning from the legends of your industry?

_____

_____

_____

_____

_____

_____

_____

_____

_____

_____

_____

_____

_____

_____

_____

_____

A Look Into The Greatest Moment Of My Sales Career

Chapter 2: My Greatest Moment

Throughout the years, I have met with many truly great sales professionals from different industries, different parts of the country, and different backgrounds. Over time, I discovered that they all had one thing in common. Each and every one had experienced a defining moment in their career that completely changed the way they did business forever. In fact, that one moment changed their life.

I didn't know it at the time, but about ten years ago, that defining moment had that kind of impact on me. It was a moment that came about through the orchestration of principles and strategies that I have been implementing now for more than twenty-five years. It required research, planning, instincts, practice, follow-up, and guts. And it all came together in front of one of the wealthiest families in the country.

Here's how it happened.

Like many of you, my sales practice was comfortably growing, year in and year out. I was already producing at a high level.

"So, why push for more?" you ask.

Hopefully, your answer is the same as mine and the reason you're reading this book. I'm addicted to the daily adrenaline RUSH of achieving great things *every day*. I believe every great salesperson is basically wired the same way. We all live for the moment, the RUSH, and the sale.

Based upon my fundamental need to reach new heights every day, I made the decision to pursue a family headed by a highly recognized and very influential entrepreneur. But there was a slight catch: the family already had a long-time relationship with one of the country's most successful financial advisors.

So, who was I to take on the mission of meeting this family?

My instincts told me it was my time to take a giant leap of faith. It was a leap of faith that marked the beginning of what would become my greatest moment.

Through research, I discovered this family was represented by an accounting firm with which I had developed a relationship over the years—referring literally hundreds of clients to the firm but, unfortunately, very few to the person responsible for working with this family.

Leveraging my relationship with other members of the firm, I was soon in front of this key partner, gathering background information and working to establish a strong enough relationship to be provided with a formal introduction to the family.

I have to admit I was a bit nervous about asking this family's CPA to consider introducing me to this family. The meeting began with a lot of small talk and catching up. After our little bull session, the discussion went from friendly to serious. "Bob, what did you want to meet about?" he asked.

I had practiced over and over in my mind how I would be confident and straightforward with my request for an introduction. My goal was to let him know, humbly, that with or without him, I was going to meet this family—but I would appreciate his help.

Most likely he would say he would think about it and get back to me, although he could say that when the time was right, he would mention me to his client. Best-case scenario, he would be excited about making the introduction.

I thought through every possible response he might give and practiced my reply to each response. Except one.

"No."

It wasn't so much the "no." I was prepared for that. It was his ensuing lecture that caught me off guard. He railed on and on as to why it would be a complete waste of my time, and I should not even try. I felt like I was being disciplined for even thinking that I could help this family!

I have always been one to keep my composure and maintain a professional demeanor, but I just about lost it! Here I am, sitting with a partner in a firm in which I had a tremendous reputation and to which I had referred hundreds of high-net-worth families. I had obtained just about every prestigious credential available to my industry. I knew I was more than qualified. I could not believe that I was not only being told no, but that I was foolish to even think about it.

Fortunately, I maintained my composure, and incredibly, as I left, the CPA told me how much he appreciated the business I referred to his firm and invited me to drop by any time. As I drove back to my office, I replayed that meeting and his message over and over again to get my arms around what had just happened. I was frustrated, hurt, and disappointed, and I began to consider that he might be right.

However, once I got back to my office, I was on to my next move: find another trusted family advisor. After numerous phone calls, I discovered that an existing client of mine knew the family. As a private banker for one of the most prestigious money management firms in the country, he and his family had been friends with my prospect family for years. Another meeting was set.

My goal for this meeting was to find out as much as I could about both the family's business and the family itself. As we talked, my angle—my value-add to the family—became apparent. The father was the true pioneer of the family's wealth, and the financial advisor worked specifically with him. They were friends and very close in age. But his three children, who were in their early thirties, were also very active in the business, each very wealthy in their own right; and none had given much thought to their own financial affairs. And THAT was my opportunity. The financial advisor had a business relationship with the father—but not the children.

I was encouraged by my newfound information. I knew I was on to something. After the meeting, I called my client again to see if he would be willing to set up a meeting with this family. As it turned out, he not only was willing, but would also attend the meeting to introduce me.

Days prior to the meeting, I developed my presentation. I knew that I would have about fifteen minutes to speak. I was told that the father and his children would be present. It was critical to clearly identify the ultimate goal. I already concluded that the father's business was unapproachable, so I set out a strategy for establishing a relationship with his children: on an age basis, I could relate to them better than their father's financial advisor; his advisor had ignored the children's needs up to this point; and they would soon be in control of this family's fortune. My presentation was built on the premise that I would impress upon the young family members the importance of choosing an advisor now, so they could begin planning for their financial future.

It would be vital to impress the dad without threatening the relationship with his financial advisor. Ultimately, I wanted to obtain Dad's blessing that it was a good idea for them to find their own advisor and then motivate the children to meet with me. That was my strategy, but I also had to make sure that I left them with an unforgettable message. I will share that defining statement with you as we get further into the actual meeting.

The evening before the meeting, I took great care in what I was going to wear. That morning, I felt like my heart was going to jump out of my chest. Part of me knew I had to settle down, but the other part loved the RUSH. There were two things going through my mind: one, I was made for this business, and two, I wanted to feel this RUSH every day.

I got to my meeting thirty minutes early and sat in my car for one more rehearsal and a quick prayer. I met my friend in the parking lot and thanked him again for setting up the meeting.

We were ushered into the large conference room to meet all the attendees. To my surprise, the conference room was packed. In attendance was the family, key executives, and support staff. My client walked in before me, and I followed close behind. The first voice I heard directed to me was, "What are you doing here?" I looked up and could not believe it was the CPA I had met with, who had told me not to pursue this relationship. Two things were immediately running through my mind: one, I should have considered that he might be there; and two, I couldn't believe he just greeted me that way!

That exchange took all of three seconds, and it totally disrupted my focus.

My client could sense my moment of utter surprise with the CPA being there and his inappropriate greeting. He gave me the time I needed to get my head screwed back on by making small talk with the family.

I maneuvered myself to sit right next to the father, as I wanted to send a subliminal message that I was confident in his presence. As my client introduced me to the family, it became my time to perform.

I was amazed at that very moment how you can, within a second, shift into another gear that reflects the confidence and ease of a true professional—the zone. I knew I was prepared and confident with my skills and ability to deliver.

If you are a successful sales professional, you can relate to the out-of-body feeling that the stage is all yours and now it's time to perform. We go into some form of high-level auto pilot.

I began by thanking the family for the opportunity. I also let the family know that I knew their CPA and had done business with his firm for many years. I was gracious in mentioning him and hoped that he would at least confirm that his firm had confidence in me. I looked at him as I was saying this and thought he would say something to help my cause. He never even looked at me and said absolutely nothing. I knew at that moment I was on my own and to forget that he was even present.

I made my presentation and explained all the features and benefits of my services to the family. The meeting was going quite well, and I knew that I was on my game. As I was coming to a close, I knew that I needed to make a statement that would leave my mark on this meeting. I knew that what I wanted to say may not be taken well by the father, and it was a risk. It was now or never. I had nothing to lose and only one chance to make an impression. I decided to go for it.

I looked directly at the father and said, "I have done my homework on you and your family. I know that you have an excellent, long-term relationship with your financial advisor. Your advisor is one of the very best in the country. I'm not here today to convince you to do business with me, because you are in great hands. I'm here because I believe your kids need to choose their own advisor whom they can relate to and have confidence in."

I could see in his face that he was impressed that I had the confidence to address him and respected his relationship with his financial advisor. The father was accustomed to salespeople aggressively pursuing him and was surprised that I was not there for him. I then looked at the three kids and made a very bold and confident statement.

"Your father has chosen one of the best financial advisors in the country to assist him with his financial affairs. Each of you need to follow his lead and select who you believe can assist you."

It was time to release my secret weapon. I continued by addressing the kids and said, "I know that it would be easy for you to use the same financial advisor as your dad. Your dad's advisor and I have the same credentials and very similar experience. But there is one thing that your dad's advisor cannot compete with, and that is my age."

There it is; I said it. I paused to let my statement sink in. The only two people in the room who were uncomfortable with my statement were the father and, to my surprise, my client who brought me to this family.

The father leaned forward, looked me right in the eyes, and said, "Son, that was dirty pool."

I responded with a very composed response: "I'm sorry you feel that way, but it's a fact. Your children need a financial advisor whom they can relate to—someone who can work with them as they grow and mature in your business. Your financial advisor is over sixty years old and will be retiring soon. I'm the perfect choice for your children."

The father sat there, staring at me, as he chewed on his unlit cigar. He stood up and called the meeting to a conclusion. As I thanked him again for the opportunity to meet his family, he put his hand on my shoulder and said, "What you said was dirty pool, but I respect your point."

No one else in the room heard him say that to me. I shook hands with everyone else in the room, then told the young family members that I would be in touch. As my client and I walked out to our cars, I could tell he was a little concerned. I asked him what he thought about the meeting. He responded by graciously saying I did a great job. But I could tell something wasn't right. I asked him how he felt about my statement concerning the age of the father's financial advisor. He paused, then said, "I'm not sure if that was appropriate to say."

I asked why, because it was a fact. My friend couldn't really answer my question, but he again expressed that it may not have been appropriate. I thanked him again for setting the meeting and walked to my car.

The drive back to my office was quite interesting. I was feeling about every emotion possible. I was livid about the CPA's attitude, thrilled with my presentation and composure, proud that I was bold with my statements, confident that the kids understood my recommendations, concerned that I may have offended the father and that I may have embarrassed my client. But my overwhelming feeling was utter pride in myself. I don't ever remember feeling such an extreme RUSH of adrenaline.

I spent the last hour of my day reflecting on every element of that meeting. This experience was the premise and inspiration for writing this book.

Oh, by the way, I wrote $50 million worth of life insurance on the younger family members. We have a tremendous relationship and have become friends. This family has also referred me to other similarly wealthy families. My client who introduced me is blown away that I now represent this family and respects me even more for my guts to go after the deal. The relationship with this family has propelled my business to a level I never could have dreamed of. The ability to accomplish this goal has given me the confidence to move my practice to the ultrahigh net-worth marketplace.

The tools, discipline, and personal lessons I learned from this experience and relationship are used every day in my practice. As you continue to read, each chapter addresses an important element of this deal and my ongoing success as a sales professional.

I sincerely believe these tools can launch your sales career to extreme levels. I also believe that by utilizing the strategies that I will share, your ascent can begin immediately.

You will notice very quickly that my thoughts are not new-age, fashionable techniques. My strategies are built on old-school, fundamental, and proven methods brought to us by the legends of the sales industry. While some strategies may not be easy, they are effective. It takes discipline and faith in yourself to achieve greatness.

Chapter 2: Questions to Consider

- Have you ever experienced a truly exceptional moment in your sales career?
- If yes, have you reflected on all of the skills you brought to that moment?
- Do you continue to bring those skills to all other meetings?
- Why are you reading *RUSH*?
- Are you addicted to the daily adrenaline RUSH of achieving great things every day?
- Have you decided to make a giant leap of faith in your business?
- How do you handle objections? Do they motivate you?
- Do you give up easily?
- Do you know with confidence that you are made for this business?
- How would you evaluate your meeting preparations?
- Do you leave a mark in your meetings—something a prospect will not forget?
- Are you intimidated by other professionals?

_____

_____

_____

_____

_____

_____

_____

_____

_____

_____

_____

_____

_____

_____

_____

_____

_____

Our Future Begins And Ends, One Extreme Day At A Time

Chapter 3: Seize the Day

There is nothing more valuable than the day you have before you. Think about it. There is not a guarantee for any of us to have anything more than the moment we have right now.

Early in my career, I was always looking to the future. Back then, I was taught by my manager to develop a one- to three-year business plan. This plan would reflect my annual income goals and be broken down into quarterly and monthly commission goals. Then, we would begin designing our marketing plan and finally our action plan, which reflected our weekly and daily prospecting goals.

I loved designing plans. I put a tremendous amount of time and thought into them and was often recognized for those efforts. Unfortunately, once produced, they were never touched. My intentions were good, but there was no follow-through.

It was an incredible waste of time! As a result, my career was not particularly dynamic. My income would plateau for two or three years and sometimes even decline. I would be frustrated and depressed. Something had to change, but I didn't know what or how.

That's when I began studying my industry's sales legends. How did they organize their time? What was their secret? As I began to read their books, I discovered a very simple and straightforward concept. Their long-term planning consisted of committing to their annual income goal. They said nothing about annual business, marketing, or action plans. For them, their focus was totally and completely on *the day*.

I was so inspired by the simplicity of it all. It had nothing to do with long-term strategies or plans. It had everything to do with activity and managing the day.

Once I understood that, my career changed. It was then that I stopped listening to managers and consultants and began following the wisdom of those who made a living by delivering results.

Today, my business plan is written when I get into the office in the morning. My goal is simple: touch as many people as possible. However, like my mentors, I do spend time on one form of long-term planning—committing to an annual income goal. Once that's established, I immediately break it down to what am I doing today.

Here's how it works.

Commit to a realistic annual sales goal and then break that number down into months. If your goal is to make $500,000 annually, your monthly goal will be $41,700. So, each week you will need to close enough business to generate $10,400 in commissions. If you average a $3,500 commission per sale, you need three sales per week. That is the math you need to know.

My days are built around how many people I must call, meet, and close. My peak time is between 8 AM and 6 PM. The only times I commit to service and case preparation is before 8, during lunch hours, and after 6.

Try it. I challenge you. If you reach out to your prospects and clients for one full day utilizing my schedule, I guarantee you will have an extraordinary day. Why am I so confident? First, because I have personally seen my income more than double since I started using this methodology. And second, it's a methodology that has proven itself for generations.

I think we can all agree that the key to every salesperson's success is predicated on how many qualified people we touch each day. You must commit to a level of activity that will produce enough contacts that will lead you to enough closings to meet your annual income goal. It's that simple.

Personally, I manage each day differently. On Monday, I focus only on setting appointments. I will not let any other activity distract me. Tuesday, Wednesday, and Thursday are committed to meetings. Any free time is dedicated to additional calls, service, and case preparation. Friday mornings are made available to product vendors.

I will only meet with salespeople who are trying to introduce me to their products at that time. I selected that time to focus on new ideas for my clients. I find it interesting that all of my vendors recognize this and respect how I control my schedule. Unfortunately, many new vendors tend to disregard my schedule and never get an appointment. They have no idea how much revenue they are missing. The rest of Friday is left for meetings and calls.

The point I'm trying to make is—*control your schedule.* There is no way to meet your activity goals each day without being disciplined and diligent with your day.

Now here's a very important point for you to consider. If we go back to the very essence of *RUSH*, our goal is to find key moments in each and every day that create an adrenaline RUSH. The RUSH confirms, drives, and validates us. You and I can only find that RUSH when a contact is made. Think about that for a moment. You and I cannot accomplish our income and activity goals unless we are in contact with a potential buyer.

The RUSH we seek may come from calls, meetings, or closing sales. I don't know about you, but I still get excited about securing a meeting. I also get a RUSH even if the call leads to no meeting. "No" does not steal my enthusiasm. To me, a "no" means I tried. Knowing that I'm doing something that only a few people have the guts to do turns me on.

I have literally made hundreds of calls in a day and never made an appointment. What a RUSH that is. I sincerely mean this. Going home, I know that I have given my absolute very best. I know that very few people would have had the discipline and drive to do that. I also know that the numbers will work out for me. It only takes one yes to make my day a success. Any more, with my experience and reputation, it doesn't take that many calls to set my week. Longevity and experience have their benefits. But that wasn't the case earlier in my career. I realize things do change and am ready to re-establish that rigor in order to make my numbers.

Having said that, I will have to admit that early on in my career, I would come home completely disgusted with my day. I would take it out on my family and sit around feeling sorry for myself. If you are feeling this way, you will find out, as I did, that it's nobody's fault but your own. The only solution to your funk is to change your tomorrow. Go in tomorrow and commit to an extreme day of prospecting. Your only goal is to contact as many people as you can to secure appointments. You may not set one meeting, but you will respect yourself. If you do set a meeting or multiple meetings, you will find your RUSH, along with new enthusiasm.

The only thing you can control is the moment you are in right now. When you ask yourself, "What should I do next?" the answer should always be the same: contact someone. A sale cannot be made when you're alone.

I would argue that our future begins when we get up in the morning. Make the most out of your day and forget about thinking long term. Everything you do must have the opportunity to produce a result— *now*. Long-term thinking is really nothing more than a daydream. Daydreamers are everywhere. I meet them every day and can predict their future. There are very few people with the discipline to follow the basics. The basics work today. They have worked for generations before.

The bottom line: as sales professionals, we are performance driven. We are wired to be in the moment, craving our daily RUSH. We cannot be successful if we are not contacting prospects. So, I need to be blunt. If you are not challenged or excited about contacting prospects, you are not made for this business.

One last thought for consideration.

Today's salespeople have lost their nerve. They are looking for an easy path to success. Once again, I need to be blunt. It does not exist.

While prospecting via e-mail, networking, or mass mailing may work for you, quite honestly, it is usually a sign that you are not comfortable with doing the basics. While you are pressing buttons and licking stamps, I'm making calls. While you're busy marketing, I'm talking to your prospects. I will guarantee you, my results will be superior to yours. It is very difficult for them to tell me no. I have developed exceptional telephone skills, and my prospects are sincerely impressed with my message.

You may feel offended by my comments. I'm okay with that. If you choose to ignore the facts, it only makes my prospecting more effective. Pick up the phone and make contact. I encourage you to give it a try. The absolute, fundamental truth to sales success is to manage and control your daily activity. You have a choice: either maximize your day or continue to be a daydreamer. There is no better

RUSH than knowing you gave everything you have as you leave the office. You will respect yourself and experience what only the very few have—success.

Chapter 3: Questions to Consider

- Do you look to the future or focus on the day?
- Has your income reached a plateau or peaked?
- Is your business strategy simple or complex?
- Who do you study or emulate?
- Do you commit to an annual commission goal?
- Do you break this goal down to the week?
- How many people do you contact per day?
- How committed are you to prospecting?
- How do you manage each day?
- Do you take pride in your current efforts?

_____
_____
_____
_____
_____
_____
_____
_____
_____
_____
_____
_____
_____
_____
_____
_____
_____

How To Find And Manage Your Adrenaline Rush

Chapter 4: Adrenaline Junkie

The world is desperate for cheap energy. Yet every year, there are more than 16 million storms throwing out lightning bolts that typically produce several hundred million volts of electricity. But it's all for naught. At least for now, we can't seem to harness the energy.

And so it is for sales professionals. We are often energized and driven by the natural RUSH of adrenaline, but have no clue on how to harness the very thing that powers, energizes, and drives us. Like lightning, our energy is gone in a flash. However, for us adrenaline junkies, there are answers!

First, let's understand from a scientific perspective what an adrenaline RUSH is really all about. The adrenaline RUSH you and I feel is accompanied by an increase in endorphin activity. It's not some mystical experience that only a few profess to have. It's real, scientifically proven, and available to us all. You have probably experienced the RUSH of adrenaline when you were frightened by something or were told to give an impromptu speech. You know what I'm talking about.

You may well have entered the sales profession not really understanding your natural desire and need to feel that RUSH. But if you are not feeling an adrenaline RUSH at least once a day, you are doing something very wrong.

The adrenaline RUSH we seek is nothing new. Adrenaline is real, natural, and something that has been recognized and studied by our industry legends.

Don't believe me? Take a look at this piece written in 1925, *The Psychology of Selling and Advertising* written by Edward Kellogg Strong:

Nature of Emotion

Cannon tells us that under the influence of the emotion of fear and rage the heart beats more rapidly, blood pressure rises, and breathing becomes deeper and also more rapid. The blood is driven out of the entire digestive system to the heart, lungs, brain, and muscles through the contraction of the blood vessels in the digestive system, and their dilation, particularly in the muscles. Sweat may break out on the skin, thereby preparing the body for rapid elimination of heat and waste products following excessive muscular activity. Such changes constitute the fundamental basis of emotion. But the mechanism is even more complicated. There are two small glands, situated near the kidneys, called adrenal glands. They also are stimulated. And they pour into the bloodstream a chemical called adrenaline. This chemical affects the various internal organs directly. It stimulates the heart to greater activity; it causes the blood vessels in the stomach and intestines to contract and those in the muscles to dilate; it causes the stored up sugar in the liver to be poured into the blood to be used as fuel for the working muscles; it eliminates consciousness of fatigue; and it even goes so far, apparently, as to put the blood in such condition that it will clot more rapidly than usual if the body is wounded.

What man experiences when emotionally excited is the sum total of the consciousness of all these bodily changes. And apparently whether he is excited because of fear, rage, or love, the body is prepared for the maximum expenditure of muscular activity.

The above constitutes what might be called the physiological side of emotion; the psychological or conscious side is hardly understood at all. But it is clear that the conscious differences between fear, rage, and love cannot be explained as Cannon has described emotion; there are other elements that must be included.

So, that was the view back in 1925. Nothing has changed. By putting yourself in difficult, uncomfortable, challenging, stressful, exciting, or important situations, you get that RUSH of adrenaline. In the world of sales, those experiences can be found in making a big call, going to see a new client, closing a profitable deal, or making a presentation to an executive committee.

So if you are not challenging yourself on a daily basis, making big calls, setting new client meetings, and closing deals—what are you doing?

I live for the daily adrenaline RUSH and, if possible, as many as I can handle in a day. I believe it is the very thing that separates us from the competition. Every day, we have a choice when we come to the office. We can challenge ourselves or let the day challenge us. We can be proactive or reactive. From twenty-five years of experience, I can tell you that proactively controlling your day will lead to profitable results. You and I have multiple opportunities to challenge ourselves by controlling the activities we choose to engage in. The following are key activities that I do every day to find my RUSH and move my firm to an extreme level of profitability.

Each day begins with the most important activity that you and I have available to us—making calls to prospects who we believe will buy from us this week. These calls take guts and confidence and can be challenging to make. But they are the difference between making money this week and not. Starting each day making the calls that make the money gives me a total RUSH.

Contrarily, many people start their days by reading the paper, talking to associates (who are also not making any calls), and returning easy calls. How productive is that? Is that the way to start an exciting day? To be extremely successful, start your day by making the most difficult and profitable calls you can make. That's a RUSH.

Next, after I finish making all of my money-making calls, I begin making prospecting calls. The difference between truly successful sales professionals and mediocre ones is in the discipline and motivation in making these calls. Personally, I find them to be the hardest thing I do. That's why there is tremendous value in carrying over the energy and momentum from your money-making calls to make your prospecting calls.

After my calls are made, it's off to appointments. My goal is to have at least three of these a day. Meeting new people is what I am made for. I love it. It's what gives me my ultimate RUSH.

As I drive to the meetings, I begin to feel the butterflies building up. I rehearse my introduction and think about what their needs may be, what they will be like, and what objections will confront me. When I walk into their office, I'm on auto pilot. It's hard to explain, but it's very similar to being in the zone. It is very natural for me to meet someone new and get them to talk to me. The whole experience is really a psychological experiment. The goal is to leave the meeting with a commitment for another meeting. The sense of accomplishment that comes from understanding your prospect's needs, having the potential to deliver a solution, AND securing a next meeting is a tremendous feeling—a RUSH that you won't soon forget.

I understand that making calls and attending meetings is not easy, but the difficulty and challenge of these activities is the very reason we get our RUSH from them.

We salespeople cannot escape the fact that we are emotionally wired. We need to feed and manage our *daily* need for the euphoria that comes from the flow of adrenaline. Your goal is to find what emotionally charges you. Once you find it, you must learn how to manage it. Once managed, you are in control of your emotions and your RUSH. Imagine. You are in control of the very thing for which you once only hoped. WOW!

Chapter 4: Questions to Consider

- Are you energized and driven by achieving the natural RUSH of adrenaline?
- Do you acknowledge that you may have entered the sales profession not really understanding your need for the RUSH?
- Do you put yourself in difficult, uncomfortable, challenging, stressful, exciting, or important situations?
- If you are not putting yourself in challenging situations, what are you doing?
- Do you challenge yourself or let the day challenge you?
- Are you proactive or reactive?
- Do your current activities feed your need for an adrenaline RUSH?
- Do you need to analyze your unproductive activities?

_____

_____

_____

_____

_____

_____

_____

_____

_____

_____

_____

_____

_____

_____

_____

_____

_____

_____

The Attitude, Confidence, And Boldness Of A Sales Legend

Chapter 5: Being Bold

First, I would like to acknowledge that making the decision to be in sales is a very bold move. Choosing this profession defines you as an individual who wants to be in control and compensated for your own performance. Many will question your sanity of working without a guaranteed salary, having to find your own clients, being rejected more times than not, working long hours, and not having any corporate ladder to climb. I can remember the disappointment in my father's eyes when I told him I was going to pursue a sales career in the life insurance industry. He could not understand why I did not want to work for a major company, earning a salary with benefits. His generation was all about the security of big employers, a consistent salary, small annual raises, benefits, and a retirement plan. I respect my dad and appreciate all that he and my mom did for me, but just think about that philosophy in today's world. Even big employers can go out of business, lay off employees, and slash salaries and benefits. There is absolutely no loyalty, guarantees, or any type of predictable future.

You and I are in a very different position. We decided to be in control of our own destiny. While others may question our decision, we know with confidence that they may have a fixed salary, but we have unlimited income potential; they have to work with clients they are given, but we can find the clients with whom we choose to work; they may only get rejection from their boss, but we only need one yes to earn what they get paid in an entire year; they may have fixed hours, but we get the opportunity to make our own schedule; they may have the opportunity to move up the corporate ladder, but we have our own ladder to climb. You should be very proud of the bold move you made in choosing the sales profession. I know that my dad now understands my profession and is very amazed and proud of me. That alone means everything.

So, with that being said, what's our next move?

Being bold, in my opinion, is a combination of confidence, attitude, and action. All three elements are critical. Every key selling element must be addressed with a bold attitude every day. It's what separates those who just make it, those who are mediocre, and those who perform at extreme levels.

You must be confident in yourself. People want to do business with people who are confident in what they are doing. Your clients and prospects can and will read it in your eyes and in your tone of voice. They can feel it in your presentation and recommendations. If lack of confidence is an issue, you must address this now.

Next, you must have a positive and optimistic attitude. Why is this so important? You and I are in the business of rejections and objections. We know that every day we are going to hear no more often than we hear yes. Almost every deal is met with objections to our product or service. Our job is to overcome the "no's" and meet every objection with an appropriate response. It's a dance that you either love or hate.

I happen to love the dance and have the attitude of a winner, whether I win or lose. Yes, you are a winner even if you lose. You must never forget or doubt this concept. You brought a solution to meet your client's needs. It's their choice whether they implement your recommendation or not. If you presented your product to the best of your ability and sincerely believe in your recommendation—in my mind, you are a winner. You cannot control the decisions your prospects make, but you can control how many presentations you make. If you maintain an optimistic and positive attitude, you will make many sales. Once you choose to become defeated, you are.

Last but not least, you must put your boldness into action. Boldness without action leads to unemployment. As I stated earlier, activity is everything in our business. In Chapter 4, I addressed the key activities you must embark on every day. Make your money-making calls with boldness. You must make those calls with the presumption of, "*When* would you like me to come out and pick up the check?" Nothing else should enter your mind. You must make your prospecting calls with an attitude of, "*When* would you like to meet?" You must approach each and every meeting with a confident, optimistic, and professional demeanor. If you bring boldness to every activity, I promise you will leave your day with tremendous pride and will have satisfied your need for a RUSH. Anything less than bold will produce disappointing results.

Quite frankly, this isn't something that gets measured by the number of sales. I *never* evaluate my days based on sales made. That can be a trap. You can have an absolutely lazy day and simply luck into a sale. You can also attack your day by doing every key activity with boldness and come up empty. Personally, I will take no sales from doing everything right over luck on a lazy day anytime. An extreme day of hard work will lead to many sales in the future. Luck will not. It will be important for you to understand this principle. Lazy salespeople who are lucky every once in a while do not last long. Those who boldly perform all of the key activities *every day* will enjoy a very profitable career.

Let us now address how to be bold in choosing your markets. We were all new to the sales profession at some point. We came into the business with incredible dreams of success. Being in control of our future and income was exhilarating. But then came the first meeting with our sales manager, who wanted to know, "What markets do you want to pursue?"

The answer to this question can make or break a new salesperson's career. It is a crime when a manager allows a new salesperson to choose a market in which they will likely fail. A new salesperson typically has more confidence in themselves than they should. I know I did.

When I was asked, I chose doctors, CPAs, and attorneys. My manager said, "Those are great markets. Let's get to work." Looking back, my manager should have told me I wasn't prepared, as a new salesperson, to pursue those markets. For months, I tried my best to get in front of these professionals. It was the most frustrating time in my young career. I had no business entering the financial business by trying to get into these difficult markets. I was broke, lost all confidence, and considered leaving the business. This was my manager's fault. I was doing everything I was told with little success.

My first year in the business drove me to crime. Every day around lunchtime, I snuck into my parents' house to make as many bologna sandwiches as I could eat. My parents caught on to my poverty-stricken lifestyle. After a while, my mom would leave sandwiches for me, attaching encouraging notes for me to hang in there. I cannot tell you how humbling that was. Thanks, Mom. To makes things even worse, my car was repossessed that year.

If you are going through this type of experience now, take my mom's advice—hang in there. While these experiences were not much fun at the time, they built the very foundation that has led me to the career I now enjoy. They made me tough, fearless, and appreciative of being committed to my decision to make it in sales.

Sorry for the long-winded story of my earlier days, but I hope it will inspire you to hang in there when times get tough.

Back to choosing your markets; I believe you must pursue several markets. I think it is critical to have at least one market that will challenge you. Every year, I try to lift the level of the markets I work. Being bold, confident, and prepared to pursue the high-end market is a RUSH. Just one deal can change your entire year. But it has many challenges. One must be bold to even consider the high-end marketplace. The decision for me to pursue this market was fundamentally based upon the following questions:

- Do I have the educational background to compete?
- Can I relate and communicate my value proposition?
- Is there a need for my products and services?
- Are there enough high net-worth customers in this market?
- How do I find these customers?
- How can I capture their attention?
- Who is my competition?
- What makes me different from my competition?
- How much of my time do I want to commit to this market?
- And the most important question: DO I, AND WILL I, HAVE THE BOLDNESS TO WORK THIS MARKET?

You must ask yourself these questions when pursuing any market. The answers will be critical to your decision to move forward. You can spend days asking and answering these questions for any market—but only the last question really counts. If you do not have the boldness to pursue the market you choose, your exercise becomes meaningless.

Whether you sell real estate, pharmaceuticals, financial services, automobiles, or whatever, when you enter a new market you will invariably find salespeople who feel they "own" that market. Early in my career, I was quite intimidated by those who controlled the markets I wanted to enter. They had worked hard to penetrate, capitalize, and dominate these markets. Who was I to step in and say, "Move over!" This alone kept me from working markets I was very interested in.

The high-end market may be the toughest. The big boys can be brutal at protecting their turf. At the time, I did not understand how to move into these markets and did not want to upset the power players. Now, I can respect how these individuals got to where they are, but I fear no one. Every market needs a new player elbowing their way in. It keeps those who think they control the market on their toes. Ultimately, it's great for the market because it creates competition and new ideas.

But be prepared to be bullied by those who are insecure about their control over your new market. I have found that those who fear my presence, and like to huff and puff, are really not worth worrying about. It is those who are truly confident in their skills and market control that you need to study. Please notice I said to *study*—not worry about. I have found that a competitor who doesn't care who I am or what I can accomplish is someone I want to learn from. I have gone as far as meeting with them to introduce myself. I have always been stunned by how professional and humble these individuals are.

To be honest, it is even more intimidating to meet someone of this caliber who only wants to help you succeed. Now *that* is boldness at its highest level. Many of these individuals have worked and controlled their market for years. Some are getting older and will soon retire. They know that someone will be taking over their market and truly respect your confidence to meet them. These opportunities do not come often. A meeting with these professionals can provide you a lifetime of information.

At some point, with hard work and a lot of humility, you will become the one to control a market. It will become your responsibility to conduct yourself in the same manner as your predecessor did. You will have the opportunity to pass the torch as professionally and humbly as they did.

This opportunity should be your vision moving forward. Boldness is a key to becoming a successful salesperson. Boldness without humility is a danger to your future and a disgrace to our industry. The business of sales is not for the weak; you must go bold or just go home.

Chapter 5: Questions to Consider

- Are you bold?
- Do you appreciate that you are in control of your compensation?
- Are you performance driven?
- Do you care about what others think?
- Are you proud of being a sales professional?
- Are you confident in your sales skills?
- Are you positive and optimistic?
- Do you believe in your product or service?
- Do you conduct yourself with boldness in all activities?
- Are you bold enough to pursue markets that others may control?
- Do you believe you can be bold but still humble?

The Biggest Time Wasters Of Today's Salesperson

Chapter 6: Death by a Thousand Distractions

When it comes to sales, there are three fundamental truths.

Fundamental Truth Number One: There are no shortcuts to a successful career in sales. While you and I are always looking for a better, faster, cheaper way to sell, it has yet to be invented. Period.

Fundamental Truth Number Two: The sales profession is not for the weak. Often, the only things we have to show for our long hours and hard work are rejections—lots of rejections.

Fundamental Truth Number Three: Anyone who tells you that the sales profession is easy is someone who hasn't been there or done that, or they're lying.

The fact is, more than 90 percent of those who enter the sales profession fail. Ten percent of those who do make it will outperform 90 percent of those who are hanging on for dear life. So, what are the 10 percent doing? Well, the real question is: What should the 90 percent NOT be doing?

What they shouldn't be doing is allowing themselves to be distracted. They're getting sidetracked by the latest gimmicks, fads, and schemes that are out there promising results without a lot of effort.

The four biggest distractions in our business today are professional networking groups, online networking, mass mailings, and seminar selling. I've tried them all. They robbed me of valuable time, tarnished my confidence, cost me untold dollars, and left me defeated.

I know. There are a lot of people who will loudly disagree. But it takes a lot of people to make up that 90 percent. My assessments are based on *my* experience, *my* results, and *my* study of what the truly great sales professionals do—day in and day out. Remember the 10 percenters?

In disbelief? Well, let me cover each of these distractions and provide you with a much more productive alternative.

Professional Networking Groups

First, I'm not talking about industry-specific groups, professional associations, charities, or organizations like chambers of commerce. I'm talking about those groups that are created specifically for the purpose of attendees generating business leads from one another.

I can remember when these groups first popped up in my professional community. At the time, I was rather new in the sales profession—working a lot, making very little, basically struggling, to say the least.

The concept of becoming involved in a group of business professionals who were highly motivated to meet other highly motivated professionals seemed to make so much sense. The only thing a person had to do was bring business cards and a handshake. This I could do.

I remember my first meeting so clearly. I wore my best suit (the only one I had) and entered the meeting with confidence. As I began to circulate, I met a number of people who appeared to be very excited to meet me. I thought to myself, "How fortunate I am to be the only financial advisor in the state who knows about this." Then I met another financial advisor and then another. I also met real estate agents, a car salesman, a pharmaceutical rep, two insurance agents, a stockbroker, and a beauty supply salesperson. Everybody, except one (a hairstylist), was a salesperson.

Undeterred, over the next three months I continued to religiously attend my networking group meeting. Each meeting was the same: more salespeople—all of whom had some very striking similarities. We were all young—very young—almost everyone wore the same clothes they wore at previous meetings (maybe I wasn't the only one who had only one suit, two ties, and a pair of worn shoes), nobody owned their own business or could speak of financial success. I tried other networking groups over the next couple of years, but found the same results.

I never met a business owner or high net-worth individual at one of these meetings. NEVER. And why would I? What's in it for them? Absolutely nothing!

Now don't get me wrong, I respect those who attend. They are at least trying to make something happen. Even more, I respect those who quickly figure out that they're a waste of time and move on.

What's an alternative? If networking in large groups is your strength, consider identifying a specific industry or geographic territory in which you would like to focus your prospecting efforts. Then go out and find organizations that serve those interests. As mentioned earlier, you will likely find industry-specific associations and groups, professional associations, and chambers of commerce—to name just a few.

I consider these organizations to be very different from professional networking groups. They are filled with successful business owners, professionals, and accomplished individuals. Typically, they share a common specialty or industry focus. Geographic organizations will typically share a passion for their community. But in any event, being a member takes a lot more than a pocket full of cards and a handshake.

Find one of your clients who is a member and ask to be invited. Attend one of their meetings and hang tight with your client. Have him or her introduce you to others and get to know the nature or focus of the group. Ask yourself, "Are these the type of people I can work with and help? Can I bring value to the organization?"

If so, get involved. Be sincere and invest your time in getting to know these people. Get to know their needs, how they do business, their personality profiles, and who your competitors are.

Indeed, your competitors will be there. These are the kind of places that the big dogs work. Give them respect. Get to know them, if possible. Study how they work the meetings and how they get involved. Keep in mind that there is always room for someone else who can bring value to the members. It will take time and hard work to establish yourself among these groups, but it will be worth it.

Now contrast that with spending your time meeting salespeople in professional networking groups. What's a better use of your time? What's the profit potential? What will give you a sense of pride? Personally, I think the answer is quite clear. Get involved!

Online Networking

I'll have to admit that technology has never held much interest for me, but I appreciate what it can do. That's why my office is loaded with the latest technology. Unfortunately, many sales professionals are relying on today's technology to do their heavy lifting—prospecting.

Does it work? Sure! For the 90 percent. Let me explain by giving you a real-life example and an alternative.

I have a dear friend who has been in sales for most of his career. Now laid off, he has started a consulting business. I recently visited his home to check on how things were going. He was very excited to see me and share his newfound passion.

He began to explain how he had been encouraged by a friend to try this online networking site to launch his new business. He was convinced that this would be very lucrative.

Out of courtesy, I sat and listened … for two hours! He said he had linked with more than 7 million "contacts" in just one month. He then began showing me all of the people he had contacted, those who had access to him, and how he had developed a Web page with all of his information.

I was just about to go crazy, so I asked to see his inbox. And there it was. Completely empty. Not one response. Zero, zip, nada.

Even with my skepticism, I'll have to say I was a bit astonished by the absence of any inbox activity. I tried to convey that he would likely see similar (hopefully not THAT similar, though) results if he continued on the same path and suggested he try something else. But he said, "No thanks." And as of this writing, he continues on in both his efforts and his unemployment.

What a shame. But it's very predictable. Online networking is a very passive activity, and prospecting is NOT passive. If my friend would have given me a few minutes to explain, I would have told him about a much more productive way to exploit his passion for technology.

Instead of spending time attempting to network with strangers, leverage the technology to multiply your reach with existing clients and prospects (during nonproductive times, of course).

The first step is to get your clients organized into a database so you can sort and categorize them by any number of common characteristics. For example, I have categorized my clients into three simple categories:

my "A" clients are my most profitable, high net-worth relationships, who receive periodic informational pieces that will be of interest to them; my "B" clients are successful relationships, who will receive information that will assist them in becoming an "A" client; and my "C" clients are those who will most likely never become an "A" or "B" client, but nonetheless receive information.

These contacts often lead to additional business. Repeat business is the easiest sale you will ever make. The next-easiest sales come from using these touches to ask for referrals. If you are not strategically staying in touch with your clients, your competition will.

By being similarly selective, you can create a database of prospects for meaningful and proactive touches.

Let me be clear: online marketing on its own is not productive. You must view it as a part of your overall go-to-market strategy. Balancing online marketing, attending association meetings, and direct telephone contacts will establish you as a recognized resource in your market.

Mass Mailing

Mass mailings have been a marketing tool for years. I have met with many sales professionals, both in and out of my industry, who market only through mass mailings. A couple of them have done quite well using this approach, but most have had very little success.

The obstacles are many. Number one, technology has made it much easier and affordable to use electronic mail as an alternative. Two, I don't know about you, but my mailbox is stuffed with marketing letters every day. Hoping your piece will stand out among the masses of other marketing literature is quite daunting. Three, and perhaps my biggest concern, are the related costs in terms of time and money.

So, what are the costs? Let's see. The time it takes to write and design the letter, to get pre-approvals (especially if you are in a regulated industry), and then for someone to print, fold, stamp, and stuff the mailer. And then, of course, there's postage. Total it all up, and it becomes very difficult to rationalize the project, especially when you take a look at what you get in return.

Based on my research, the average response to a mass mailer is about a half of a percent. So one must send out 1,000 mailers to get five responses. Of those five responses, three may set a meeting with you. Of the three meetings, one or two may eventually lead to a sale. There's no control over if or when someone might respond. I'm a control freak, always looking for a RUSH. I cannot think of a more uncontrollable and boring activity in which to participate.

How many successful sales professionals in your industry send out mass mailers? None of my industry's leaders do.

So let's discuss an alternative. In my professional opinion, there is no better way to get an appointment than picking up the telephone and calling. When you think about the time and costs involved, there's no contest. Making quality calls will outproduce a mailer any day. I guarantee it.

On my worst day, I can secure one appointment for every ten contacts made by phone. On the other hand, at least 1,000 mailers have to be sent to secure one appointment. My cost will be zero; your cost will be substantial. Your prospect will be unqualified; I will have already spoken to mine. I can also do research on my prospect prior to my meeting; you have no idea who your prospect is.

So let's take the math out a bit further. I can make fifty calls and secure five meetings; you must send out approximately 1,000 mailers to obtain five leads. I can make fifty quality calls in four hours; your mailer will take, from beginning to end, several days. The math and results of making direct quality calls cannot be argued.

Now, let's discuss what I mean by "quality calls." First, a quality call for me is a referred lead. I ask every new client for referrals. I typically average three referrals from each new client. If I average three new clients a week, that will produce a minimum of nine referrals. My personal success rate of securing a meeting with a referred lead is 50 percent. So I can typically secure four to five meetings a week from nine referred leads. You will have to send out 5,000 mailers to even have a chance of achieving my results.

If not a referred lead, the next level of quality prospecting call I make is to a warm lead. A warm lead is a prospect who is part of a market I control. For example, if I participate in an association that I'm recognized in, I will call prospects within that association. My call script will be well prepared before I begin. I will make sure the prospect understands that I'm a member of their association and knows about my involvement. I will also communicate that I represent many other businesses that share their same needs and challenges. My last proposition statement will include a service or product that I know will be of interest to them. Finally, I close by asking for an appointment. You will not believe how many appointments I can secure with this approach.

If I can convince you of anything, commit and work hard on obtaining referrals. Quality referrals each week will replace the need to send mailers. Making prospecting calls embodies all of the elements of finding your RUSH and financial results.

Seminar Selling

I'm not going to spend a lot of time on this time waster. Seminar selling has many of the same elements of a mass mailer. As a matter of fact, most seminars are preceded by a mass mailer to attract attendees. The time, cost, and results pale in comparison to quality prospecting calls. Many people attend these things for the food. In fact, I have very wealthy clients who tell me, point-blank, they are there for the free meal. Maybe that's how they became so wealthy?

My alternative to seminar selling is the same as it would be for mass mailings.

Bottom line: distractions such as professional networking groups, online networking, mass mailers, and seminar selling can all be replaced by simply delivering quality products and services to your clients, staying in touch, servicing their needs, and asking for referrals.

Now my final question: How many of the sales leaders in your industry whom you would like to emulate deliver quality products and services, stay in touch with their clients, provide excellent service, and ask for referrals? The answer: ALL OF THEM.

Think about what you are doing. Ask yourself some hard questions. Be honest with yourself. And emulate what the greats are doing to build a successful and gratifying sales career.

Chapter 6: Questions to Consider

- Do you think the sales industry is easy?
- What are the top 10 percent revenue earners doing that you are not?
- What are the other 90 percent doing that they should not?
- Are you among the 10 percent or 90 percent?
- Do you believe that professional networking groups, online networking, mass mailers, and seminars are a waste of time?
- Have you ever met a successful business owner at a professional networking group?
- How has online networking worked for you?
- Have you ever calculated how much time and money a mailer really costs?
- How many people at your seminars are there only for the food?
- Are there better uses of your time than what you are doing today?
- How many sales legends of the past and stars of today conduct business by utilizing these time wasters?
- Are you ready and willing to go back to basics?

Are You Made For This Business? Be Prepared For The Truth

Chapter 7: Uncomfortable Yet?

Well, here we are. It's gut-check time.

After covering a lot of territory, we have reached a major crossroad. From here, as long as you are true to yourself, any direction is fine. I'm hopeful that you are ready to join me for the rest of the journey, but given the statistics we talked about previously, I realize that for many, this chapter may be the end of the road. Let's face it; not everyone is cut out to be a salesperson.

If you have reached that conclusion, congratulations and good luck! Sincerely, if you don't have the feelings about this profession that I have discussed up to this point, you will likely be much happier and successful in any number of other professions.

The reason most people get this far in the book is that they think they have what it takes, but something is not quite right about their sales performance. "They're not hitting on all cylinders," as some would say.

So what about you? Perhaps you're in a rut and need to find a way out. You know that you have so much more to give, but can't figure out why you're not. Maybe you have never really learned the basics and feel somewhat lost or frustrated. Or perhaps, as I mentioned, you're not really sure if this business is for you.

My goal is to help you figure this out. Please fasten your seatbelt. There is some serious thinking just ahead. And then right after that, we will get into the really serious stuff for those who are willing to implement the hard-core activities that have made sales legends, well, legends.

Let's begin with *the* question: "Why did you choose sales as a career?"

For me, there are a number of reasons. One, I have always been very competitive, and a sales career fulfills my need to be challenged by others. Two, I want to be in control of my own destiny. Three, I love the idea of an unlimited income potential. Four, I know I have the self-discipline (now) to do what it takes to thrive in this business. Five, I can handle rejection—it motivates me. And, last but not least, I enjoy working with people and solving their problems.

You must ask yourself these same questions NOW. If any one (or more) of these six questions does not reflect who you are—that could be a warning flag. Don't gloss over it. Think about it.

As I have repeatedly emphasized, sales is very tough. If you are working hard and yet just eking out a living, something is very wrong. In my opinion, there must be a significant financial reward to compensate you for the demands of this business. Think about it. The problem could be the compensation structure. It could be the product or service. It could be you. Be brutally honest with yourself. Either step up or move on, because being a sales professional and "just getting by" are mutually exclusive.

Quite frankly, many struggling salespeople have just simply accepted mediocrity. They will never professionally achieve anything more than what they have today. If you are content with your income and activity level, seriously, put the book down. There's nothing more here for you.

If you truly desire greatness and are willing to accept that you may be one of the obstacles getting in your way, the following thoughts may help you further evaluate whether you truly have what it takes.

The first six chapters of *RUSH* established the key attributes of an exceptional sales professional. Quite simply, we are wired very differently than most. We have a natural craving that can only be satisfied by the daily RUSH we get from taking a risk, going big, and making a sale. The emotional roller coaster that it takes to achieve this RUSH is just icing on the cake.

If you cannot relate to the daily need to feel the RUSH, you must listen to your mind and body. If you don't have an insatiable craving for the immediate energy that this business can deliver, if the daily emotional highs and lows are too much, it's time to reassess.

We have also addressed the need to be disciplined in attacking each day as if it is your last. If you live for the now—for the thrill of the moment—you can control your future in sales. If you are a long-term thinker, a strategist, and like to plan every step you take, reassess.

If you can't imagine a day without an adrenaline RUSH and will do whatever it takes to find one, you are in the right business. If you have no idea what an adrenaline RUSH is or have really never experienced one in your daily activities, reassess. The RUSH we seek is addictive and part of our very being. Is it part of yours?

If boldness is part of your nature, and you strive to stretch yourself every day, you are made for greatness. If you struggle with confidence and can't imagine pushing yourself beyond your daily routine, reassess.

Do you strive for the feeling of being completely dialed in, operating in the zone, building the momentum to sustain strong performance levels? Is the idea of parlaying high-level activities, one on top of another, motivating? If yes, read on; if no, reassess.

So, have you reassessed everything so far and still think you've got what it takes? But as you glance out the window, your career is nonetheless plodding along in the right-hand lane of the freeway—often drifting below the speed limit—and maybe over onto the shoulder now and then?

I have been there! For years! Mindlessly going nowhere in particular. Stop 'n' go. Always stuck behind someone. Aaugh! Grab the first exit! Get into the high-speed lane! Do something!

Unfortunately, many people don't. Why?

Well, I have had this conversation with myself many times. Believe me, I can relate to every excuse, problem, and misconception as to why someone would tenaciously camp out in the right-hand lane, content with mediocrity. If you know that you have everything it takes to be a huge success in sales, why do you choose not to live up to your potential? You should be embarrassed, disgusted, and ashamed of yourself. I know that I was. And it took those feelings to wake me up. Unfortunately, nobody had the guts to tell me I was failing myself and family.

I sincerely wish someone would have taken me by the collar and challenged me to get off my butt and get to work. I hope you know that I care enough about you by writing this book to get in your face and speak the truth. If you are willing to accept that there are no excuses and are ready to make significant changes, there are a few key decisions you must make before you can go anywhere.

Number one: Remove yourself from negative, unproductive, whining salespeople in your office. If you have your own office, shut your door. Do not hang out with, associate with, or spend time with unproductive, negative sales associates. Remember, once you remove yourself from this group, you will be ostracized by them. Be prepared for gossip and nasty remarks sent your direction. This is a good thing and will serve as a confirmation that you're moving in the right direction.

Number two: Find others in your office (or, if necessary, outside your office) who are producing the type of income you want and associate with them. Study their habits. Ask if you can attend meetings with them. Listen and watch everything they do. Take notes and incorporate their strengths into your practice. Read and study what they read and study. Mirror their hours and commitment to working hard. Ask how they market and prospect. You will be shocked at how differently they conduct their prospecting activities. Osmosis will take place, and you will act, feel, and be different.

Number three: Get your financial act together. Salespeople are typically a financial mess. I can very clearly remember needing to make a sale today to pay my bills tomorrow. The pressure of being broke oozes into your client meetings. Your prospects can feel your desperation to close the deal now. You must get your debt under control, establish an emergency account, and have the discipline to pay your bills on time. Having financial peace of mind will enhance your closing presentations. Your goal should be to WANT every deal, not NEED every deal.

Number four: Take the time to study how your mentors project their image. What type of clothes do they wear? What kind of cars do they drive? How do they handle themselves in social settings? Are they humble? How do they convey what they do for a living? It's important for you to, as much as possible, emulate how they project themselves, although keep in mind that you are not yet at their income level. Do not emulate them so much that you go into debt. You must do all you can to project a successful image without destroying yourself financially.

Number five: If you have never been one to read and study, you must begin now. Every successful sales professional I know is an avid reader and very committed to their education. Most regulated industries have credentialed education programs. Credentials send a clear message that you are experienced and committed to be an expert. Enroll in a credentialed program NOW to separate yourself from your competition.

Number six: Get up early Monday through Friday. Successful sales professionals are up early and ready for their day while most are still in bed. You must be willing to commit to planning your day before your prospects get in each morning. Your goal is to hit the day fully prepared. Control your schedule and let no one interrupt. Finish your day after all your prospects have left. If you get calls at 5 PM, you must be available for them. Mediocre sales professionals come in late and leave early. Separate yourself from them by being prepared and available *every day*.

Number seven: Find your RUSH. Find the activities that turn you on. Do the activities that most will not. Repeat the fundamentals every day to create consistency. Study yourself and ask what is motivating you throughout your day. Enjoy the drive to the bank to make deposits. Take pride in paying your bills on time. Cram as many adrenaline-producing activities into your day as you can handle. Live for the RUSH and never look back. Be humble in your newfound success. Help others to learn your secret of success.

One last point: I will admit to you that for many years of my career, I was lazy. I possessed all the skills to be dominant in my industry. I had huge dreams and worked harder than most, but did not fulfill my potential. Like most salespeople, I'm not great at making and keeping personal and professional long-term goals. My commitments to myself are typically good for about a week, and then I fall into old habits.

I sincerely believe that a lot of my past mediocrity was based upon my misconception of the value of long-term goals. I'm just not wired to make, commit, and stick with long-term changes. Perhaps you can relate.

Once I discovered the power of planning and living for the day, my career exploded. If we can agree that long-term planning doesn't work for you and me, and we are open to a new approach, then why not try short-term planning? Commit to performing at an extreme level for one day. Once that day is over, try it again tomorrow. Planning for an extreme day is the essence of *RUSH*. Commit to trying this concept and be prepared to be shocked.

The result of parlaying one extreme day after another will create momentum in your work. Once momentum begins, you will find that work and deals will find you. It's all about activity. The more people you touch, the more work you will find. The more deals you participate in, the more referrals you can ask for. The more clients you obtain, the more repeat business will follow. Your business will begin to grow beyond your wildest expectations. You will begin to receive random calls from people who have been referred to you daily. A day doesn't pass that I don't receive a call for a new potential deal. And it all began by working smart and hard for one day.

In closing, this may be the last page many of you will read. I may have offended you by now, challenged your desire, or confirmed your thoughts of leaving sales. For those who must leave now, good luck with your future. I mean this sincerely. For those who are convinced that you are made for this business, let's get to work. See you in the next chapter.

Chapter 7: Questions to Consider

- Can you relate to what you have already read in *RUSH?*
- Are you made for this business?
- Why did you choose a career in sales?
- How is your sales performance today?
- Do you understand the sales basics practiced by the legends?
- Are you 100 percent committed to do what it takes to be successful in sales?
- Are you in a rut?
- Are you competitive?
- Do you enjoy working with people?
- Have you chosen mediocrity?
- Have you ever really felt a RUSH?
- Do you want to feel a RUSH every day?
- Are you prepared to study the legends of your industry?
- Are you committed to education?
- Do you live for the day?

_____

_____

_____

_____

_____

_____

_____

_____

_____

_____

_____

_____

_____

_____

_____

_____

_____

Emulate The Greats Of Your Industry And Become A Legend

Chapter 8: Seek Out Your Industry Legends

Do you golf? Play tennis? Shoot hoops?

Are you so good that if you magically had a day on the course with Ben Hogan, Jack Nicklaus, or Tiger Woods, you wouldn't learn anything new? Would advice from Arthur Ashe, Bjorn Borg, Venus or Serena Williams be meaningless? Would Michael Jordan be unable to match your ability for taking it to the hoop?

I thought so.

Well, what about that same kind of opportunity, but with a sales legend?

I tried it. And it changed my career. COMPLETELY!

I find it extremely interesting to compare the practices of sales legends with what the superstars of our industry are doing today. You will be shocked. The FUNDAMENTALS HAVE NOT CHANGED. Take a look at the quote below.

> *"The salesman's function is to make him [the customer] realize his wants and show him how to find satisfaction."*

Hello? Anything new here? And there probably wasn't anything new about it when *The Psychology of Selling and Advertising* hit the bookshelves in 1925.

Unfortunately, finding someone in your industry worthy of emulation may not be as easy as studying Tiger Woods's swing.

My first ten years in the financial services industry were quite challenging. I was surrounded by mediocrity, but didn't know it. I was often one of the best-producing sales associates in my office. My manager would often tell me just how great I was doing, but I couldn't pay my bills. After a while, however, it became clear. He was really saying I was the least pathetic of the bunch.

That was frustrating. So I started looking around for sales professionals whom I could learn from and emulate. But clearly, where I worked, the well was very dry.

Without anyone to learn from, I turned to reading everything on sales and marketing that I could get my hands on—thus triggering my addiction to reading. To this day, I read one to two books a week.

At the time, I had no idea of what to read, so I began with self-help books. I desperately needed some self-motivation. And while those books helped me better understand myself and lifted my spirits, what really needed a lift was my sales performance.

So I moved on to reading every new release that came out on the subjects of sales and marketing. To my surprise, I began learning things about my profession that were never taught in my office.

Let me digress for a moment.

In looking back, sales offices can only offer so much education. In my opinion, they are often run like a child daycare center. The manager's job is to spoon-feed the basics and raise salespeople through their adolescent years. Eventually, a salesperson has to make a choice: grow up and move on, or stay put in the safe haven and remain a child. A sales manager can never teach you anything more than what the home office passes down. There comes a time when you have to take the responsibility to learn more on your own.

Okay … now I'm back.

I devoured just about every sales and marketing book available. They helped. My income started to increase, but at a moderate pace. Something was still missing. They didn't tell me exactly how to become an extreme producer in my industry.

But then, a MIRACLE happened. The absolute perfect book landed on my desk: *Ideas Are a Dime a Dozen*, by Joe Gandolfo. This gentleman is a legend in the life insurance industry; he began selling insurance in the early sixties. Unlike the newly released books that were generally written by sales consultants or managers (which should have been my first clue!), Gandolfo's book was by someone who had "been there and done that" better than just about anyone. He told me exactly what he did, day in and day out. My career changed the day I began reading his book.

It was like finding the fountain of youth; I was reborn! Which, like any addiction, led me to seek similar books and, from that, to find Frank Bettger. He wrote a book called *How I Raised Myself from Failure to Success in Selling* (first written in 1949, by the way). Again, I was astonished by how much I learned. And now here's the real irony. You can pick up *both* of these books on Amazon.com for less than $5. Five bucks! I just think about the thousands of dollars spent on training programs where I first worked.

The best part of these books is the simplicity of their message. These gentlemen had one goal: touch as many qualified prospects as possible—*every day*.

With that, I made the commitment to study and emulate *everything* they did. The following are the valued lessons I learned and now practice EVERY DAY.

But before we begin, think about this for a minute: without a cell phone, Blackberry, e-mail, voice mail, or even a computer, they met and spoke with more people than you or I could ever imagine on our best day. Now *that's* what I'm talking about!

One of the first lessons? Preparation. These guys didn't go out on their first sales call until they memorized their introduction presentation. And then they memorized responses to every objection that could possibly come their way.

Common sense?

Come on, let's be honest. Do you have an introduction presentation down cold? Or do you just kind of wing it? Quite frankly, up to that point, I was pretty much freestyling most of my meetings. I was overconfident in my ability to communicate my services and too lazy to really commit anything to memory. It's our nature. We get lazy and think we are better at our craft than we really are. It may sound a bit remedial to go back to such a fundamental aspect of our business, but once I did, my income jumped. You can't argue with results.

So humble yourself and develop a new introduction. Commit it to memory and measure your results over the next thirty days. Now, I can understand that you don't want to be robotic in your presentation. I'm not saying that's what you have to do. Just take some time and really think through your value proposition. What makes you different? What unique skills do you bring to the relationship? What makes your product or service superior to others? Study your new message. Practice it. Deliver it with precision.

Have you ever had the opportunity to sit in with a truly great salesperson and listen to their introduction? I have. It's magical. Clients can't resist. You will never be able to fully evaluate your presentation until you hear one of these masters perform. Take this advice very seriously. It's a game changer.

Next, these legends were masters of controlling a meeting. Think about how hard it is to obtain a meeting and yet how little effort goes into the meeting itself.

The legends fully understood and appreciated that everything they saw and heard as they entered a meeting was a potential clue into the interests, passions, and desires of the person they were about to meet for the first time. Their radar was on full alert. Nothing got past them.

As great salespeople shake hands, they are assessing if their prospects are analytical, expressive, amiable, or a driver. I hope these personality profiles bring back memories. In just seconds, they are deducing any number of things and are able to spontaneously begin asking questions to match those deductions.

Again, I have had the opportunity to sit in with some real sales pros. Through insightful questioning, they control the meeting and gain valuable information. They understand that the typical person thinks that he who does all of the talking is in control. So they let them! And all the while, these masters are sizing things up and taking inventory on how to present their value proposition.

The absolute best-of-the-best will allow their prospects to open, close, and sell themselves. It's amazing to watch and listen. Simple questions like, "What can I do for you? What do you want in a provider? What type of product/service are you looking for? When would you like to purchase or begin? What do you like, or don't you like, about your current provider?"

Not only do they allow people to sell themselves, but they deliver their message in a manner that is consistent with their prospect's personality profile. If their prospect is analytical, they will deliver the perfect presentation incorporating the details that an analytical person would appreciate. If they're a driver, the legend will deliver the exact sales message touting bottom-line solutions. You get the picture.

Do you do this? I know I didn't.

I was like so many salespeople who think they need to talk in order to control the meeting. We are so enamored with ourselves that we cannot shut up. We want to tell our prospects who we are and how wonderful our products are. We end our meetings by typically asking our prospect, "So, what do you think of our product?"

I would be so embarrassed, and I hope you are too, to leave a meeting without a sale and with absolutely no idea of what the client really wanted.

The legends were also relentless prospectors. They relied on just one piece of technology—the telephone. These pros were masters on the phone. Again, they prepared a script that clearly stated their value proposition. They also prepared for every objection that could come their way.

They had times in their schedules dedicated to prospecting. They would pick up the phone and call until their week was full of appointments. And I mean *full*. To the tune of twenty-five to thirty appointments a week! When's the last time you did that?

In his book, Gandolfo offers this little piece of math on which you can chew. If two salespeople start in the business on the same day and one sees twenty-four people in a week and the other sees twelve, the former will be twice as experienced (and probably make twice as much money, I might add) in just one year. The person seeing twenty-four people a week will accomplish in five years what it will take the other person ten years to achieve.

The simple truth is the legends were more committed and worked harder than most people can ever imagine. The point here is very clear and simple: if you aspire to be one of the greats in your industry, you must step up your prospecting game.

It's by no coincidence that all of this coincides with the very thing we have been talking about since the beginning—the RUSH. Acting with boldness. Producing results. *Every day!*

Are you willing to commit to that? Remember, you only have to commit to one day at a time. Try it and evaluate your results. An extreme day of prospecting will lead to a full week of appointments. This experience will become an addictive RUSH that you will crave every day.

The legends were also committed to education. They took pride in their profession. It was vital for them to learn everything they could about their product or service, and they would enroll in education programs to obtain certifications in their field of expertise. They were so committed to being a credentialed expert that if you were not, they would challenge your commitment to the business—right there in front of your client.

Originally, the education thing was a huge issue for me. I had become very good at prospecting. It came very naturally, and I loved the RUSH it provided. My problem was that I was getting in front of big clients, but did not have the education to provide much value. There is nothing worse than obtaining a great meeting with someone and not having any meaningful ideas to offer. This left me with two options: bring someone with me who did have the experience and split the commissions, or get educated.

Option one was not appealing to me at all.

Typically, there are seasoned veterans in the office with tremendous product knowledge and no motivation to do their own prospecting. They will literally sit around and wait for new reps to ask them to assist with their meetings. How depressing is that?

They loved me. They saw my energy and would literally fight over who was going to mentor me. They wanted to be my buddy, showered me with praise, while living off of my commissions. But, I had no choice. I needed their brainpower.

After reading Gandolfo and Bettger, I quickly enrolled in my first certification program. It took me three years to obtain my first credential. I was so proud and can remember my wife making me a cake with the credentials inscribed in the frosting. Since then, I have obtained four additional designations, and I'm working on my sixth.

Again my income took a leap. The results were undeniable, as I used (and continue to use) the exact same strategy as those before me. I ask a prospect to show me the card of their current provider, and I zero in on their credentials. I have yet to come across a competitor who can match my credentials. And when I point this out to a sincere buyer—SOLD!

How are you doing with your education? If you are truly committed to greatness, you MUST step up your commitment to education. Enroll in a program that your clients will recognize and respect. TODAY!

These are just a few of the lessons I have learned through my study of the legends of my industry. There are sales legends in every industry. Your job is to find yours. Ask around; seek the advice of a sales pro who you respect. Chances are, they already have the books on their shelf and will lend them to you.

As I mentioned earlier, I find it extremely interesting that today's great salespeople have become that way by emulating the legends. I'm fortunate to know three extremely successful financial advisors whom I compete against in my region of the country. They have allowed me to meet with them and pick their brains. I cannot emphasize enough that all three of them practice the fundamentals *every day*.

Their businesses are actually quite simple, but very profitable. They are also very humble, extremely professional, and highly credentialed, and they work harder than most. They are amused by all of the gadgetry that everyone is clamoring over nowadays. They see none of it as a threat. They are fully aware that there is only one person nipping at their heels—me.

Everything I have learned has come from the legends of my industry. They were the inspiration for me to write this book. I wish I could thank them all personally. It is my sincere hope that someday this book will be referred to as the source of inspiration to others who achieve sales greatness.

Chapter 8: Questions to Consider

- Do you know who your industry legends are?
- Have you ever read a book by or about one of your industry's legends?
- Are you interested in meeting a sales legend?
- Have you ever met one of your industry legends?
- Who do you respect today in your industry?
- Can you set a meeting with that person?
- Do you know what questions you would ask?
- Do you know that today's sales stars emulate the legends of the past?
- Are you bored with advice from today's consultants and sales management?
- Do you have a convincing proposition statement?
- Do you feel effective in your new prospect meetings?
- Do you ask a lot of questions?
- Are you committed to working as hard as the legends?
- Are you obtaining industry education certifications?
- Do you ask for referrals?

_____
_____
_____
_____
_____
_____
_____
_____
_____
_____
_____
_____
_____
_____
_____
_____
_____
_____

A Diversified Prospecting Strategy That Delivers In Good Times And Bad

Chapter 9: Shooting Rabbits While Elephant Hunting

Prospecting is the genesis of our business. Poor prospecting equals even poorer sales. Great prospecting equals … well, let's just say you've earned the right to continue on, and *hopefully* you make great sales.

Unfortunately, the thought of prospecting sends the shivers down people's backs. It's by far the most difficult part of our business. Everyone struggles with it. *Everyone!* This is so ironic because, in its most elemental form, prospecting is a matter of selling yourself. And who can't do that?

So it's absolutely vital that you step back and take the time to assess your prospecting efforts. To help you, we're going to check out and let you compare the prospecting activities of sales legends with today's superstars. Between the two, you may be like me and come up with your own winning formula.

Based on everything that has been written so far, you may be surprised to learn that there *is* a difference between the sales greats of today and yesteryear—and it's their prospecting styles. I will point out the strengths and weaknesses of each and give you a sneak peek at my own prospecting structure, which is a hybrid of the two.

First, let's look at the legends. Remember, we're talking about people who did it all without e-mail, voice mail, mobile phones, or computers. Their tools of the trade consisted of primarily the telephone, some form of a fact finder (an information piece from their employer), a pen, and sometimes a car. That's it.

Time-out, for just a minute.

Think about how different our days would be without a mobile phone. To be honest, I'm a big fan of the past. I love and respect the simplicity of it all. Our 24/7 world can be overwhelming. Clients expect your cell number and have no problem calling you late in the evening. E-mails are sent to me at 1 AM. Clients expect information immediately, not in a day or two. I can appreciate the convenience of technology, but what is it doing to our sanity? In one respect, it has made our job easier and more efficient, but it often robs us of the time needed to be thoughtful in our work.

Now back to our legends.

Now that you can appreciate the limitations they had, you will be amazed by their activity and productivity. They were relentless, committed to prospecting *every day*, all day long. And although they had the same twenty-four hours that we have today, they used them quite differently.

Twelve- to fifteen-hour workdays were common for the sales professionals I studied. They were in the office by 6 AM (known as the six o'clock club), had a thirty-minute break for lunch, and then were back to work until around six in the evening. It was home for dinner and then out again for another couple of meetings. They worked on Saturdays too!

Wow! I work long and hard, but I'd have a tough time keeping up with that! But I'm sure they had their slackers too. You know, those who would just skate by on their paltry fifty or sixty hours of effort each week.

These highly successful sales professionals carved out an entire day for prospecting. They did not have access to mailing houses or any other service to provide lists. It was the local phone book, a newspaper, or an employee roster obtained from someone in a company's personnel office.

Their secret to it all? Being prepared. Their lists and scripts were waiting for them when they walked through the door. So, right from the start, it was show time! Sit down, smile, and dial. They would call until their calendars were filled with appointments. We're talking about twenty to twenty-five meetings a week! That's mind-blowing to me.

By the way, even though your industry may have different prospecting numbers than mine, I will bet that when you take a look at your industry's sales legends, their numbers will be substantially higher than yours. Sorry, but it's true!

So, what's the lesson?

If you're in a rut, you must increase your prospecting activity. If you are seeing five prospects a week, double your efforts. If you're not profitable seeing ten, double it. I know that may sound extreme, but when you're broke, extreme is the way to go. And the legends are proof it can be done!

Oh I know, it's important to have balance in our lives. I agree— except for when you're broke. Sometimes, we have to get out of balance in order to get back to a balanced lifestyle. Many of the legends I studied practiced this concept. If you are new to the business of sales or financially challenged, you must commit everything you have to get ahead. Your family will need to understand this.

Fortunately, I was single when I started my career. I just worked hard and partied hard—until I started a family. Then, I worked harder. No parties. When I married, I sold my wife on the dream of a life of luxury—and she bought it! If you saw her, you would know without a doubt that I'm a master salesman. But every time the dream of financial success started to fade, I would tell her that I had to recommit—letting work and life get out of balance. And every time that I recommitted to extreme prospecting, everything changed for the better. Once I was able to bring things back to balance, I would maintain a much more active prospecting schedule. Finally, it stuck and my financial affairs skyrocketed.

Bottom line: reassess your prospecting levels. If you don't like where you are, then double them. I told you it wasn't going to be easy.

For the legends, prospecting didn't stop when they put down their phones. They asked every client or prospect for referrals. It was either that or cold calls, and they could not reach their lofty goals by talking to total strangers. They would ask for family referrals, business referrals, and neighbors. They didn't care about net worth or profession; they just wanted to meet decision makers who could cut a check.

The legends were also very active in community activities and industry associations, where they were sure to meet potential clients. Many would become the president or a board member and give a tremendous amount of time. They cherished their profession and took great pride in how they could help others. Their integrity and humility conveyed their message for them, providing them with significant business. If you can communicate this type of passion, referrals will be a piece of cake.

Finally, the legends ensured that a portion of their client mix included the high-end marketplace. But they would only pursue these markets after they were incredibly trained and confident they could add value. They would find their high-end prospects by studying the newspaper, asking for referrals, volunteering their time, and everyday prospecting. They would meet with a wealthy business owner and didn't give a second thought about going next door to introduce themselves to another wealthy individual. They were so confident and had no fear. I love that!

All I can say is, study your legends and prepare to be humbled. Emulate them and prepare to become wealthy.

Now, let's look at today's sales superstars.

A lot has changed—the tools of our trade, our products, the markets, our customer's expectations. The high-end salesperson of today has had to adapt.

I have had the opportunity to spend time with three of the most successful financial advisors in the country. It was truly a pleasure and an eye-opener to see them at work.

While they all have cell phones, two of them rely completely on their staffs, who work in very high-tech offices, to handle all of their technology needs. This is quite in contrast to many of today's sales professionals, who conduct meetings using laptops. To me, laptops interfere with the relationship-building aspects of our business. The superstars don't need these tools. They appreciate the value of personally connecting with their clients. All they need is a meeting and a need, and they can sell the product conceptually.

When it comes to prospecting, today's sales pros prospect through relationships—never a cold call. The phone and social gatherings are their weapons of choice. Every call they make is either a referral or someone they met at one of their social gatherings. The pros of today are typically masters of the social scene. They are extremely involved in charity events. They know that's where the truly high net-worth people hang out.

These pros are absolute artists when it comes to working a room. They do it in a way so that others seek them out. Their pitch is, "Let's get together for coffee next week." The prospect doesn't even know they're a prospect and has no idea what our sales pro does for a living. They build a network of influential people and build an incredible center of influence. It's all about being with, and being seen with, the right people.

Please understand that their prospecting is not all about schmoozing with the right people. These pros are brilliant at their profession. They are investing themselves in the actions and passions of their market and contribute significantly in terms of time, money, brainpower, and experience. Many are so committed to their cause they actually run their own nonprofit organizations—working hard, raising money, and inviting future clients to their fund-raising events. Everyone wins!

What can we learn from today's sales pros?

First, it takes time and a lot of work to become a master of sales. These individuals, like our legends, have committed to a lifetime of learning. They are typically credentialed and experts in their field. If you have any aspirations of becoming a player in your industry, you must commit to becoming a credentialed expert NOW.

Referrals are the key. They must become a part of every conversation you have with a client. You're not asking for charity. You are owed a referral as a result of your hard work. Sales pros believe that every client should be honored to introduce their friends and associates to someone who can add the same value to them. They expect and earn every referral they receive. Sales professionals of our past and present have understood this fundamental principle. Strong relationships build trust, trusting relationships create business. Once the relationship is built on trust and respect, referrals will come. Ask and you will receive.

Next, consider participating in a charitable organization. You will find that these organizations are full of wealthy, well-intentioned families. If you choose to become involved in a charitable organization, you MUST be sincere in your efforts. The sales pros of today give so much of their time, expertise, and dollars to their charity of choice. Choose a charity that has touched your family or a close friend. It's critical that you do not use the charity as a platform to promote yourself. Serve with class, and always be a professional. Make a difference in other lives and you will be rewarded many times over.

So what are some of the differences between the stars of today and the legends? Today's superstars do not make cold calls—period. They only call on referrals and people they meet socially. Today's pros do not have the same activity goals. They may see five to eight people a week. But every one is significantly wealthy. Their school of thought is quality over quantity. They will write very few deals a year, but for significant commissions.

And now, my turn. As you can see, I'm a fan of both the present and the past. I owe my career to studying and emulating the activities, sales practices, and work ethic of my industry's legends. It has also become quite clear that the present-day pros have also parlayed what they have learned from their mentors.

From this, I have developed a hybrid strategy that takes the best of both. This may not be right for everyone, but I thought you might be interested in what I call "Shooting Rabbits While Elephant Hunting."

For me, it is critical to diversify my prospecting into small, medium, and large accounts. Every day, I try to meet with prospects who have very different financial profiles and, as a result, very different needs.

Why?

For one, I like the challenge of shifting gears from one prospect to the other. Making calls to a variety of different businesses and professionals is not easy. I think that's why I enjoy it so much. It's a RUSH and a challenge I crave.

I also think there is a huge payoff. Practice makes perfect, and prospecting to multiple markets allows me to keep sharp. Every prospect has different challenges, needs, and demands. I believe if I can handle a variety of rejections from different markets, I can handle anything. So when I do meet with a high net-worth client, I am fully prepared. Think about it, if I have seen many clients throughout the week and presented my services over and over, do you think I'm stressed out to meet a high net-worth prospect? Does my week depend on closing them? They are just another meeting (with a few more zeros).

Two, I believe a well-diversified prospecting strategy is wise in a challenging economic environment. As I write this book, we are experiencing the most challenging economic climate of our generation. A challenging economy would not have had a major impact on a legend. Sure, business would be tough; but they would just continue their same strategy, introducing their service to anyone who has a need.

Alternatively, the present-day sales pros are having challenging times. They are dependent on fewer accounts, with high-dollar commissions. The problem is that in tough times, these high net-worth business owners tend to preserve their assets and not spend money during these types of business cycles. If they miss one or two deals a year, it can be financially devastating.

I have chosen to diversify my markets in order to minimize this risk. If times are tough for high net-worth people, I just shift my time to more small and medium-sized clients. I can still pay my bills. In fact, while others are downsizing, thanks to diversification, my business continues to grow.

Three, I also diversify my practice by age and gender. There is an opportunity to sell to at least one market regardless of what is happening with our economy. If the elderly prospects are preserving their assets or not buying your products, the younger market may. If the younger market is feeling the stress of a potential layoff, the older market has a fixed income. Everyone has different needs at different times whether the market is strong or weak. I want to be in a position to shift my services to those who are capable to buy when other markets are not. I do believe high-end salespeople will soon understand the benefits of diversification and change their business to adapt. If they don't, there will be nobody left but me. And I'm okay with that.

Now that you understand why I believe in a diversified prospecting strategy, let's move on to how I do it. I have mentioned many times before that your industry may have different numbers and challenges. I respect and understand that. But please consider my strategy and plug in your numbers.

For me, every Monday is prospecting day. After I make my money-making calls, I move on to prospecting calls. No mailers. No networking groups. No online marketing. No seminars. Just me, the telephone, and my prospects.

One point I would like to make about calling prospects: I begin prospecting by calling referrals first. If I did my job the previous week and obtained referrals, my new week is filled with appointments without making one cold call. That is the norm for me. Once I complete my referral calls, it's on to warm calls. I have mentioned earlier that a warm lead is someone I have met or would like to meet who belongs to an association or group in which I participate. If I have been actively involved, these prospects will either recognize me or meet with me out of professional courtesy.

If I have any room left in my schedule, I begin to call current clients who I believe will have additional needs. I will only set up one center of influence meeting per week. They are my last call. And then I'm done. I know that sounds simple. The simplicity is in my commitment to referrals. Once my prospecting calls are made, it's off to appointments. But my prospecting doesn't stop here; to the contrary, it's just beginning.

Once I get into my car, I begin to focus on my meetings. As I pull up to my prospect's office, I begin shifting into opportunity mode. I'm very aware of neighboring businesses and make mental notes of those I may want to meet. Once I walk through the door, I'm on full alert, looking for signs of partners, executives, and family members. Again, I take mental notes and collect as many cards as I can from the front desk. I try to be discreet when doing this or will just ask for permission. Whenever I have asked a receptionist if I could collect business cards, I have never been denied. This has everything to do with my complete respect and professionalism with office support staff. After all, they are the gatekeepers to the business owner, and who knows? They could be family. You should be respectful of all. I'm amazed at how many salespeople are not.

Once I enter my prospect's office, I begin assessing their personality. If I feel they are the type to show me around, I will ask them to do so. Many business owners love showing off what they created. I can't think of a better way to meet partners and key executives of their firm. As we finish our tour and discuss business, I take tremendous notes and ask many questions. In closing the meeting, I always discuss how I get paid. Prospects appreciate this and begin seeing you as trustworthy. In talking about payment, I mention that one of the ways I get paid is through referrals. I reinforce that statement with a question: "If I provide you a service or product that meets or exceeds your expectations, will you refer me to others?"

Nine times out of ten, their response is yes. I then take one more step by asking if they would have a problem with me contacting some of their partners or executives to see if they would like to meet the next time I'm at their office. Again, typically their response is sure.

Now think about that for a moment. I have just met with this person, and they are okay with me contacting their executives (whom I probably already met in the tour). If so, when I call these executives, I remind them of our meeting, but in any event I definitely mention that I'm already working with their boss. And by the way, I will be out there to see their boss next Tuesday at 10 AM; can they see me at 11? And then on to another and another.

This is an extremely effective prospecting strategy. It gives me a RUSH every time. Give it a try; you will be amazed at the results. As I leave the office, I will typically jot down a business or two located in or around this business. If I get desperate for prospecting meetings, I will call on these people.

About associations and nonprofit meetings, I'm very selective where I volunteer my time. I have to believe in the cause to commit my time. My prospecting efforts in these organizations are secondary to helping the cause. My goal is to make a huge impact on the organization's mission, which will be seen and appreciated to the point where members seek me out.

Often, as I am being congratulated on my efforts, I will be asked what I do for a living. I keep my response vague and use the opportunity to ask them out for coffee or lunch so we can get to know each other. Again their response is, typically, "of course."

My last secret weapon is being available and prospecting on Friday afternoons. Most of the salespeople I know take Friday afternoons off. They assume that their clients and prospects are already gone for the weekend.

How wrong they are. Many of my biggest deals start with a Friday afternoon call. I have found my clients start thinking about their personal needs as their weeks wind down—so that's when they call. They are always impressed that I'm there for them. I have also found prospecting very effective on Friday afternoon, for the same reasons. Most business owners and professionals are winding down on Fridays. They are thinking about themselves and personal projects they must get to. No one else is calling them but me. They are impressed that I'm working Friday afternoon and are willing to talk to me. Give it a try; it works.

That's it. Prospecting isn't rocket science, but it is everything to our business. Almost every financial challenge you have can be solved through extreme prospecting. If you do not believe me, give me a call. Try to get through. I dare you.

Chapter 9: Questions to Consider

- How are your prospecting activities?
- Does prospecting intimidate you?
- Are you addicted to technology?
- How many hours do you work in a day?
- Do you prepare before prospecting?
- What are your markets?
- Are you diversified in your markets?
- Will your markets withstand economic challenges?
- Are you involved in associations or charitable organizations?
- Are you active in your community?
- Do you look for opportunities before, during, and after meetings with prospects or clients?
- Do you earn the right to ask for referrals?
- Do you work on Friday afternoon?

_____

_____

_____

_____

_____

_____

_____

_____

_____

_____

_____

_____

_____

_____

_____

A Prospecting Strategy For The Ultrahigh Net-Worth Individual

Chapter 10: Go Big

ARE YOU READY TO RUMBLE? Then why not step into the ring?

Picture it!

"And now tonight's feature fight. In this corner, standing six foot five, weighing 230 pounds, the defending heavyweight champion of the world. And in the other corner, tonight's challenger, standing five foot five and weighing 150 pounds … YOU!"

Whoa! Who set up this fight? Your manager? No. It was you. And while nobody expects you to last through the first round, you are already visualizing wearing the championship belt and your next bout.

Touch gloves and come out fighting!

I can't think of a better analogy for making a call on a high-stakes opportunity, whether you're facing an ultrahigh net-worth prospect, a large corporation, or a deal where millions of dollars could be on the table.

Your prospect looms bigger than life—a truly heavyweight champion in the business world. You, on the other hand, feel like an amateur, a lightweight, unworthy even to be in the ring. You look at the phone with trepidation. Circle it. Back pedal a bit. Feint a couple of attempts. Then with a deep breath, you pick it up, dial, and wait for a connection. And as you hear the call being picked up, you engage in the biggest call of your career.

THAT, my friend, is going big—making a big call to a prospect who can change your entire career. Is it worth it? Are you prepared? Can you last beyond "Hello"? Will you go down with the first question?

Actually, the real question is, "Will you even step into the ring?"

Most will not. But in fact, the sales superstars of our past and present get into the ring *every day*. They train, they study their opponent, and they relish the thought of victory. They know with every battle, they get better. They are absolutely confident with their skills. The RUSH they get from it all is natural, instinctive, and a part of their very soul.

Can you relate? Do you have what it takes to answer the bell? If you are one of the few who can envision stepping into the ring for the fight of your life—*every day*—you will need a trainer, someone who has fought these fights before and come out a winner.

There are many who will tell you they are qualified to be your trainer: your office manager, a peer, or maybe a sales consultant. But chances are they have never even stepped into the ring—let alone actually won. You need a battle-tested champion. In short, you need a legend. I cannot stress enough the importance of finding your industry's legends.

Today, going big is a challenge that I MUST engage in *every day*. I look forward to it. But early in my career, I didn't really understand this concept until I started reading about, learning about, and observing the successes of my industry's legends.

I have found the legends of the past were not as strategic in their marketing to the ultrahigh net-worth individuals as present-day legends. They would meet with just about any individual who had a need for their product or service. They committed time for marketing to high net-worth individuals but not with the same tenacity as our present-day superstars. Their strategy was to study the newspaper, identify new employers moving into their territory, and ask for referrals. Once they identified a high net-worth individual, they would simply call or go to their office and introduce themselves—without an appointment. They had guts, confidence, and pride in their ability to deliver. Their philosophy was, "Why not me?" It was simple, direct, and effective.

Today's sales superstars are singularly focused on the high net-worth market. It is very uncommon for them to meet with anyone who does not meet minimum income or net-worth criteria. They are all about the quality of their client base, not quantity. They meet their prospects through referrals, centers of influence, charitable events, and social gatherings. Cold calls are typically never made, and dropping by unannounced to introduce themselves is completely out of the question.

Based on all of this, I had a dilemma on my hands. I appreciated both approaches but could not buy 100 percent into either strategy. So I created a hybrid, high net-worth prospecting strategy that best suited my style, my skills, and today's market.

So, let's begin.

First, we need to go back to the very premise of *RUSH*. The fundamental need of every sales professional is to feel the RUSH, *every day*. There is nothing more exhilarating, challenging, or intimidating as making a big prospecting call to an ultrahigh net-worth individual. It takes guts, boldness, discipline, and confidence. If you want to feel what an extreme RUSH really feels like, you have to GO BIG.

Let's define what I call "going big." I would define this activity as making a prospecting call to an ultrahigh net-worth individual, meeting with an ultrahigh net-worth individual, or attending a social gathering with the focus on meeting an ultrahigh net-worth individual. This activity MUST be done at least once a day.

This is consistent with my strategy to stay focused on the day. My goal is to make ONE, very big contact each day—period. I can commit to that. It does not overwhelm me or feel impossible. I need to get into the ring, just once, *every day*.

Going big. How does it work and when do I do it?

Every day, through referrals or other research, I am adding high net-worth individuals to my prospect list. I select from that list and will typically ask my assistant to do some additional research so I can immediately capture my prospect's interest. In some cases, I find that my prospect may have similar or common interests as I do. If I was referred, I obviously focus on that.

You may recall that I start every day with my money-making phone calls. I then parlay that momentum into making prospecting calls. Then, and only then, will I make the BIG CALL.

I do this for two reasons. One, if I was successful making my other calls, my week is already set. I know with great confidence that my week is going to be successful, with or without a high net-worth contact. Two, after making all of these calls, I tend to be in a great rhythm—

basically, in the zone (which we have talked about before). So, I don't get up from my desk, go for a walk, or take a break. I immediately pick up the phone and make the big call.

Having that momentum is critical. Because sitting between you and the heavyweight is a gatekeeper. And getting through depends on a confident tone of voice, calm demeanor, and a simple request.

Here's what I do.

I listen for the receptionist's or secretary's name and then simply say, "Hi Tammy. Is Tom in?"

This simple introduction is very difficult to deflect. Remember, a gatekeeper's job is to prequalify every phone call coming into the boss. Politely saying, "Hi," and asking for my prospect by his or her first name suggests that I'm a friend or business associate of my prospect. The gatekeeper has just seconds to decide if my call should be screened further or simply passed on through. More times than not, I get put through.

But not always. The next question then becomes, "Who is calling?" My response is, "Bob." Again, the gatekeeper is in the exact same position of having seconds to decide if I should be let through or not. Often, that's all it takes.

But not always. The next level of screening usually goes the route of asking for the reason of my call. My response: "I'm calling to set up a meeting." And the poor gatekeeper is left with seconds to make a decision on the next step.

Not getting past the gatekeeper is often a matter of either providing too much information or having a tone of voice that lacks confidence and calmness. Believe me, it takes practice. LOTS of practice.

Once I get the big dog on the phone, it's all up to me. I have just two goals: make a quick and favorable impression, and obtain a meeting.

My introduction and proposition are short and crisp. I listen to responses very closely to identify anything that will assist me. Your job is to seriously think through your value proposition and how you can communicate it quickly and with confidence. Remember, you only have to make one of these calls a day. Can you handle that?

One thing I have found interesting in today's market is that very few salespeople are making calls to the ultrahigh net-worth individual.

How do I know? I ask them. I find this extremely interesting. Salespeople either are too afraid to call or can't get past the gatekeepers. I have also found that many salespeople will send an introductory e-mail or something through the regular mail. They are wasting their time. You will find that many of these prospects will actually respect your courage and confidence in making a call to them.

Remember, many of the ultrahigh net-worth prospects started in sales or employ many salespeople who are expected to also make these types of calls. I asked a prospect who wasn't very receptive to my call if he employed a sales force. He said, "Yes," to which I responded, "Do you expect them to make calls to prospects of your caliber?" The response was a humble "Yes." I then asked for a meeting, which he granted. I made this gentleman a client, and he respects me very much.

Making calls of this type takes a lot of boldness and guts. Do not be afraid to be strong or to challenge them professionally. Many of these individuals are looking for someone to earn their time.

So one way of going big is to make one big telephone contact *every day*.

Another option is to go big by meeting with an ultrahigh net-worth prospect. If you are not going to make a big call today, you MUST have a big meeting secured for the day. This meeting must be so big in comparison to your everyday typical meetings that you are extremely excited. This will be the RUSH you are looking for.

These meetings call for significant preparation. You must gather as much information on your prospect as possible. Study their business and know their competition. Go to your centers of influence and ask if they know your prospect. Look for association or charitable relationships. You MUST go into this meeting with as much information about your prospect as possible.

Then begin to prepare your introduction and proposition statement. Rehearse them. And then rehearse them again and again until they're second nature.

I will often write down notes on key points that I want to make and study them. Next, prepare your introduction materials—brochures, business cards, and any other informational pieces that you think might be of interest.

When I prepare, my last step is to see if any of my clients work in the same industry or are involved in similar activities as my prospect.

Typically, I will find two or three. I call them and ask if I may let my prospect know that I represent them. My clients appreciate being asked and sometimes actually know my prospect well. In my meeting, I will let the prospect know that I have asked for my client's permission to acknowledge my relationship with them and encourage them to call my client as a reference check. The prospect respects my sensitivity to confidentiality and is typically impressed with my client base. This activity begins to build their trust and confidence.

It is not easy to obtain meetings with ultrahigh net-worth clients, so you must make the most of this opportunity. Be prepared. No. Delete that. Be *over* prepared.

Open your meeting with a sincere thank you for his or her time. Begin by asking a lot of questions. Your goal is to get your prospect to talk as much about his or her business and family as possible. Bring up the fact that you have done your homework. Ask about the charities in which he or she is involved. Build rapport, display your confidence, show your sense of humor, be humble, and present your uniqueness. Ask for the opportunity to show what you can do. Ask for a follow-up meeting. And finally—deliver. No. Delete that. *Over* deliver.

The RUSH that comes prior to, during, and after your meeting is the ultimate feeling you can obtain in our profession.

If your day does not include one big call or one big meeting, you MUST seek out one big introduction for the day.

I often have opportunities to attend charitable functions, social gatherings, sporting events, or association meetings that are also attended by high net-worth individuals. These environments are great. They allow you to engage your prospect on a social level, build a rapport, and then suggest a meeting in a week or two. Done!

But even at that, I'm very selective about what events I will attend. I work hard all day and typically do not have a lot of energy for after-hour gatherings. I would much rather spend my time with my family. That may sound harsh but my family comes first.

If I'm invited by a high net-worth client or a significant center of influence, I will attend. It doesn't get much better than being introduced by someone who respects you and is also trusted by the prospect. My clients and centers of influence know my motivation is to meet someone significant. They will typically tell me about a person they want me to meet. I work with them so they know how to best position me and my business. With this type of setup, I am very successful in obtaining meetings.

In conclusion, you must make a big call, or conduct a big meeting, or attend a function to meet a big prospect, ONCE EVERY DAY.

The results?

I cannot begin to tell you the positive, adrenaline-pumping results of this activity. Please understand that obtaining a meeting with an ultrahigh net-worth individual is very tough. I fail much more often than I succeed. But it only takes a couple of people to say yes to make an extreme difference in my year.

Making a big contact every day takes discipline and courage. Many of your peers will never have the guts to step into the ring. Going big just once a day provides the RUSH we seek—even if we are rejected. You see, the RUSH comes whether you obtain a meeting or not.

Additionally, as your day comes to a close, you will have so much respect for yourself and pride in your efforts. A day of challenging yourself to do all of the bold activities is a successful day—period.

Many of your big contacts will lead to leaving a message, waiting for a decision, or hoping for a meeting. What a great way to go into your next day: with the possibility of a response from a big prospect. Some will call back, some will say yes to your recommendation, and others will want to meet. Every day there are many big prospects who may call my office. Nothing excites me more than my receptionist transferring the call of a big prospect who is returning my call. It makes my day and confirms the activity.

My income has increased substantially by committing to going big every day. My bank account is all the proof I need. The income allows me to afford nice clothes, an impressive office, and a great lifestyle. Successful people want to do business with successful people. They brag about you to their friends and invite you to their private gatherings. Once you're in, you become even more productive. The results of going big have changed my career and will change yours, if you're willing to step into the ring, once a day.

An important reminder: I do not dedicate all of my time to prospecting to ultrahigh net-worth prospects. I intentionally market every day to small, medium, and large prospects. Diversification is very important to my long-term success and ability to adapt in difficult markets. I go big just once a day and will never allow this market to control my destiny.

I find working the smaller market rewarding and very humbling. I enjoy working with all types of individuals and learn from every relationship. Many of my smaller and mid-size accounts have actually led me to much larger accounts.

Well, there you go. It was a great fight. You lasted all twelve rounds with the heavyweight champion of the world. He knocked you down several times, but you got up. The crowd was roaring. Your trainers were so proud. The referee begins to tally the score. The winner and NEW heavyweight champion of the world is YOU. They place the world champion belt around your waist, and you walk out of the ring with your head held high. You're famous and everyone wants to know how you did it. You go back to your locker and reflect. And the only thing you can think of is your next big fight. Your fight has already been scheduled. Tomorrow you will walk back into your office, knowing your next contender is waiting. All you have to do is step into the ring.

Good luck, champ.

Chapter 10: Questions to Consider

- Have you ever made a really big call to an influential prospect?
- If yes, did it give you an adrenaline RUSH?
- If no, what was holding you back?
- Do you want to work with the ultrahigh net-worth market?
- How would you define an ultrahigh net-worth prospect?
- What is the difference between you and the people you know who work this market?
- Do you identify and create a database of high net-worth prospects?
- Do you fully prepare before making calls to high net-worth prospects?
- How do you introduce yourself to high net-worth prospects?
- How will you contact a high net-worth prospect?
- Are you willing to make the commitment to make one big contact every day?

How To Parlay Extreme Activities Into Phenomenal Results

Chapter 11: Enthusiasm Breeds Enthusiasm

Activity, action, and momentum are the keys to our success. Sure, skills, education, experience, and boldness are all important, but they mean nothing if there isn't any action. Let's face it. From the very first day we walked into the office, our job has always been about activity.

Managers know their number one goal is to motivate a new sales rep to make something happen—*now*. Make their calls, talk to family members and friends, attend networking meetings—*anything* that will get them to meet people. But, quite frankly, maintaining a high activity level is a challenge that just never goes away. It's just as much an issue for experienced and mid-level sales professionals as it is for the new rep. In fact, it's the single biggest struggle I have.

Activity is not something that just magically happens. We must create it—*every day*. It is our responsibility to put into place the daily activities that will produce client and prospect communications. Every day, before I'm open for business, I prepare my list of strategic activities. But making the list doesn't count as an activity, putting it into motion does.

It is through the succession of activities—one right after another—that we begin to crack the code for what makes great salespeople so great. It opens the door to perhaps one of the most fundamental, career-changing concepts that I absolutely live by: enthusiasm breeds enthusiasm. Let me explain.

The essence of this concept is to understand and manage one victory, and then parlay that success into another activity. How many times have you made a big phone call and secured that meeting, or closed a deal that you didn't think possible, or presented your pitch with complete perfection—and then stopped? We have all done it. It's only natural. We want to stop and just relish the moment. Daydream on how wonderful we are. Live the moment over and over again. Some of us can't wait to run and tell everyone just how great we were. Unfortunately, by the time we're finished running and rerunning the instant replay of our great moment, we not only have wasted a lot of time, but also have completely lost something very important to our greater success—MOMENTUM. Enthusiasm without follow-through is a wasted opportunity.

Momentum can be one of your greatest assets if you first understand it and then learn how to use it. Here's a simple example. I begin every day by placing money-making calls. As explained earlier, these calls are made to prospects whom I believe will buy from me this week. Once I secure one of these meetings, I could either bask in my greatness or inject that excitement into my very next call. Think about it: why waste time telling everyone else about your great accomplishment (*hint*: they don't care anyway) or sit in your office and revel in yourself?

The moment you secure that all-important meeting and feel the RUSH coming from your success is the exact moment that you need to pick up the phone and make another call. Your goal is to take the positive energy from one success and use it to fuel your next success. Your high-energy, positive attitude and enthusiasm will make a very positive impact on your next prospect. I have found it is very difficult for someone to deny me when I'm on a roll.

It is critical to stay focused on keeping your enthusiasm going. Be assured that you will run into road blocks. Prospects will say no. Once a salesperson's balloon has been burst, most will want to stop and ponder, "What just happened?" They will analyze the situation and go off to talk with anyone who will listen to their sob story (*hint*: they still don't care).

Why is that? We have all heard that misery loves company. When I was in an office with many other salespeople, I saw this take place every day. One salesperson down on their luck would find other salespeople feeling the same and compare notes.

All they want to do is talk about how tough things are. How nobody wants to buy their services and products. How slow it is for everybody. How they can't pay their bills. Nobody is going to buy during the holidays, so why even try? Fridays are always horrible to make calls because no one will be in. Sound familiar? How depressing is that?

It happened every day in every office with which I have ever been associated. When such people come to my office, I tell them to share their story with someone else. I have no time to discuss failure. Quite honestly, misery is infectious, and those who stay in that state of mind soon become unemployed. It is the antithesis of enthusiasm.

I thrive on being around enthusiastic people. They motivate, inspire, and lift me up when I'm down. Nobody can be motivated and enthusiastic all the time. You have a choice to join a pity party or choose to associate with those who do not accept excuses and move forward every day with excitement.

One thing I have learned is to compartmentalize my activities. Enthusiasm can only breed enthusiasm when you choose to create one positive activity after another for a period of time. There can be no interruptions. Close your door, prepare your list of calls, and make one after the other until you're done.

Here is what you will come to realize: One, you will feel a sense of adrenaline before you begin to make your calls. Use this adrenaline to your advantage. Two, once you make that first call, you'll use the RUSH to make the next. Three, now you're beginning to be in the zone. Your only focus is to make as many of these calls as you can without interruption. Four, you cannot be stopped. Your calls are getting easier and your message clearer. Five, you are having successes and failures, but it is all about the numbers and the activity. Six, you're done. At this moment, you should be a bit exhausted, but excited that you have accomplished this task and are ready to move on.

This may sound like a lot, but we have only just begun our day. Remember, we are creating momentum that needs to carry *throughout* the day. You should be pumped that you made your big money-making calls. Most likely, you were successful. But even if you did not secure any appointments, you should still be feeling the RUSH that comes from this activity.

What's next?

In my world, it is on to prospecting calls. Prospecting calls are the hardest calls for me (and maybe for you too). We all know that rejection is just around the corner, which is why there is no better time to be making these calls than when you are all warmed up and feeding off the RUSH of making money. The goal is not to lose your momentum. Don't take a break. Just switch gears, pick up the phone, and start prospecting.

Again, you must be 100 percent focused and not interrupted. Your goal is to obtain as many new prospect meetings as possible to meet your weekly prospecting goals. With phase two of your day now completed, you have accomplished the most important activities you can possibly do. After all, without prospecting, there are no closes. With a number of closes, you now need to fill your calendar with new prospects.

And with that, you should be exhausted. It is now time to take a break. Get out of the office and clear your mind for fifteen minutes.

With the hardest part of the day behind you, it's time to go on appointments. I don't know about you, but meetings are my greatest joy. My goal is to stack as many meetings into a single day as I can. The best-case scenario is to have just enough time to get from one meeting to the next.

This principle follows the concept of enthusiasm breeds enthusiasm. Performing at your very best, one meeting after another, is what feeds our craving for the RUSH. If you stack one meeting after the other, you will have very little time to ponder the outcome of your last meeting. If it was not productive, you will have very little time to reflect, because you are now thinking of your next meeting. If it was a success, you will be carrying that enthusiasm over to your next meeting. That enthusiasm should be peaking as you pull into your last meeting.

As you walk to your car following your last meeting, you should be totally spent. If you are not, you need to ratchet up your activities. There is nothing more fulfilling than knowing you have accomplished a great day. Your closing meetings are set. You have a number of new prospects scheduled, and you just met with a number of great new prospects. What more can you do in your day?

Now is the time to reflect. Most people do this throughout the day, wasting time and energy. You, on the other hand, choose to look back on your day's accomplishments without wasting a moment. You have managed and controlled the vital energy and momentum that drives you to achieve extreme results. Ironically, by *not* doing what everyone else does, you will become one of the very few who stand among the greats.

But here's a word of warning.

Those who perform at the very highest levels and do not associate with those who choose mediocrity will be ostracized. I found very early in my career that I was different from most of my peers. I began my career in an agency of many salespeople. There were many different levels of experience in the group. The one common trait I found was a sense of mediocrity. Very few worked hard, and many liked to sit around and complain. I was often criticized for not joining in. Many thought I was cocky to believe that I could actually become an extreme producer in my business. I hated being around gossips and lazy people. I was humble but optimistic. I believed I could do anything I put my mind to. Others, I believe, were threatened by my desire for greatness. Many tried to befriend me, but they were only trying to ride my coattails.

Many years ago, I decided that I could no longer be around a negative environment and started my own company. I now choose who I want to be around. I often meet with the very best in many industries and ask them how they made it to be the very best. In every case, they have relayed the concept of enthusiasm breeds enthusiasm.

And there you have it. Parlaying one success into another is their secret, and now it's yours with which to build an incredible career and lifestyle.

Chapter 11: Questions to Consider

- Is maintaining a high level of activity a challenge for you?
- Do you prepare for your activities every day?
- Do you parlay one activity into another?
- Do you understand the value of managing and creating momentum?
- Do you associate with unproductive salespeople?
- Do you schedule and manage your prospecting activity?
- Do you have a network of other highly successful sales professionals?
- Do you meet with them often?
- Are your days filled with appointments?
- How do you feel about your day when you get home?
- Do you understand that you must create and manage momentum?

_____

_____

_____

_____

_____

_____

_____

_____

_____

_____

_____

_____

_____

_____

_____

_____

_____

The Most Powerful Weapon In The Sales Arsenal: Referrals

Chapter 12: Ask and Ye Shall Receive

Earlier, I told you about my greatest moment.

But my greatest *deal* actually came about nine years before ... when I was still practically a rookie. I was such a rookie that, at the time, I didn't even realize I was using the most powerful sales tool ever invented to improve my odds. The fact is, I would have never gotten in, let alone made the pitch, without this powerful tool.

It's known as "the referral."

You see, at the time, I needed help. There was plenty of competition, and I needed someone who, through an introduction, could put me ahead of the crowd. To make a long story short, that referral got me in the door, and the woman I desperately wanted to meet ultimately said yes and became my wife. Nineteen years and three daughters later, she and they are still and always will be my most-valued clients.

So began my respect for the concept of referrals.

Take a look at any legend or present-day superstar and you will find that their success is directly linked to referrals. It's the difference between good and great—the "10 percenters" and everyone else. Quite simply, referrals will change your career. They are the solution to producing extreme sales results.

But you don't get them if you don't ask, and very few salespeople ever do. Here's why:

Some salespeople have absolutely no intention of developing a relationship with their clients. They are probably representing a second-rate product and are just looking to make the sale, collect their commission, and move on. Next! Customers can see through this in an instant. Even if a referral were asked for, none would be given.

Referrals MUST be earned. They are the result of clients appreciating, trusting, and respecting you as a professional. This takes time and commitment.

This leads us to the salesperson who has every intention of providing good service and developing a relationship with their customer, but doesn't. They represent a quality product but just can't seem to take the next step—service. Fatal mistake. Good intentions get the same results as poor execution. No service. No referrals.

And then there is the salesperson who simply doesn't ask. What? How is that possible? A good product, a good relationship, and no referrals. OUCH! That really hurts. Just a step away from greatness, and they walk away with mediocrity and an average income—just like everyone else in the office.

Maybe they're afraid to ask? Oh please, don't tell me someone has chosen sales as their profession and is too shy to ask. There can't be a shy bone in a salesperson's body. Confidence and boldness is a part of EVERY encounter. Remember, be bold or go home!

I suppose there are also industries where salespeople traditionally don't ask for referrals. They sell a product, a car for example, and never expect to see the customer again. I guess they can follow tradition. The other option is to get out of the box and do something BOLD. Remember, be bold or … oh, I already said that. Personally, I would not only ask for referrals at the time of sale, but also call a month or two later to ask how they are enjoying their car and ask for referrals again. If no one in your industry is asking for referrals, just think how much a salesperson with some boldness about them will stand out.

Bottom line, if you're an experienced salesperson with integrity who services your clients, you have earned the *right* to ask for referrals. There is no reason for you to be prospecting like new a rep.

New salespeople typically don't have the opportunity to learn about the value of referrals. It's not their fault. Sales offices spend all of their time on training us how to prospect. In working with their new reps, most sales managers are of the mentality to preach cold calling and networking. It's almost seen as a rite of passage.

It's no wonder that very few salespeople make it through their first year. I know that I was never taught how to ask for referrals. I was given a desk, a phone, and the Yellow Pages. It doesn't take long to figure out that prospecting is extremely difficult, and most will just quit. Referrals can give a new salesperson hope when prospecting is really grinding on them.

If you are new to sales, there is hope, and the solution is referrals.

I hope I have now convinced you to go out and pop the question (about referrals, that is). So when should this happen?

Answer: *Constantly!*

I make it very clear in my first meeting with prospects that obtaining referrals is one way I get paid. I tell them that I only work on a referral basis and that, as a matter of fact—that is how I met them. They respect my frankness. I then follow up with a question: "If I meet or exceed your expectations, will you refer me to others who you know and respect?"

They will typically answer yes. This prepares my future client for when I actually ask the question. Then, in my second meeting, I will ask if they have given any thought to individuals whom they could introduce me to. This is my way of reinforcing how I conduct business.

Once the deal is closed, I ask. And I receive. As my relationship grows, I ask again. And receive more.

The process then begins all over again with my client's referrals. I ask them. And I receive. Again and again, over and over. I make no cold calls. Every week is filled with people who already have some confidence in me because I was referred.

Sound too hard? Harder than cold calling? If you think so, then you are welcome to my Yellow Pages. I don't need them anymore.

Having said that, I'll have to admit there is a bit of an art to getting people to actually come up with the names and contact information for their friends and colleagues.

If you are making the effort to ask for referrals, then you are probably used to hearing the response that I often get: "I'm still thinking about who I can send your direction."

TRANSLATION: "I have not given it a single thought." SECONDARY TRANSLATION: "I hope you will not ask again."

What do you do?

Remember earlier in the book I discussed walking into a new prospect meeting with your radar on full alert. My radar is always looking for partners, executives, family members, vendors, and my prospect's competitors. Now THOSE are the referrals I'm talking about.

I acknowledge to my prospects and clients that it is hard for people to provide referrals and even harder to find the time needed to think through who they would refer. So I make it easy for them.

Once I have developed a relationship with my client and have provided value, I begin to list all of the people I know they know— whom I would like to meet. I go over the list, name by name, and simply ask if I have their permission to call them.

I am very rarely ever told no. As a matter of fact, at the end, they will often tell me I missed a few people. A little later in the relationship, I will repeat the process with a list of vendors or other business relationships. And then finally, down the road, I will go over a list of their competitors and ask if I may use their name to introduce myself.

This strategy has always been very successful. My clients expect me to ask for referrals. I make it very clear on day one and then just help them along the way. The best compliment I get is when a client says they are now emulating my referral strategy in their business.

I also receive referrals from professionals, CPAs, attorneys, and bankers. I spend a lot of time teaching them *how* to refer me. I have to. Otherwise, I get the line that they gave one of their clients my name and I can expect a call. TRANSLATION: There will be no call (if they really gave out my name in the first place).

Here's what I do when I'm told my name was "given out." First, I thank them for considering me. Then I ask if I may contact the prospect directly. I explain that it is rare for a person to actually call based on that type of referral, and if the prospect really needs my services, then they should be comfortable providing me with their name and number. Typically, they understand and respect my request. Once I have the client's name and number, I call, which the prospect appreciates. Meeting set. Sale made.

I also take a lot of time teaching my centers of influence on how to properly introduce me and what I do. I've found that they appreciate the guidance. In return, I practice what I preach. I'm a significant center of influence to those who refer me. I always provide their name and number and position them as they have requested. In providing a referral, I will typically set and attend the initial meeting to introduce both parties.

You must also give if you want to receive.

Referrals are the key to your sales career. If practiced every day, in every meeting with every client, you will be overwhelmed with prospects. Just think, no cold calls, no mailers, no networking groups, or any other time wasters. Can you imagine walking in Monday morning with twenty or thirty referrals to call? Think about all the appointments you will set.

How many sales await you?

Ask. Give. Receive.

Chapter 12: Questions to Consider

- Do you ask for referrals?
- Do you earn the right to ask for referrals?
- Do you believe you deserve referrals?
- Are you confident with the quality of your services and products?
- Is the quality of your services and products holding you back from asking for referrals?
- Do you present to your prospects and clients how you get paid?
- Do you incorporate in your presentation that obtaining referrals is a part of how you get paid?
- How many referrals do you obtain weekly?
- Do you assist your clients in identifying potential referrals?
- Do you teach your centers of influence how to refer to you?
- Do you wait for referrals to call you or do you proactively call them?
- Do you give referrals?
- Are you committed to begin asking for referrals?

A Day In The Life Of A Master Sales Professional

Chapter 13: Game On

Good morning!

It's time to get up and have the best day of your sales career. Now that you understand the fundamental concepts of *RUSH*, it's time to bring it all together. And to do that, we will dissect one day, and then one week, of an extreme sales professional. ME!

As we go through all of the concepts, activities, feelings, and results, your job will be to plug in the numbers you need to achieve your goals—and then *commit*.

Remember, your commitment to the *RUSH* strategy is for *one day*. If you have phenomenal results, commit again the next day. I can assure you that within a week of totally committing five days to the *RUSH* strategy, you will be shocked with the results. But please, one day at a time. If you can do that, let's begin.

By the way, what time do you get up in the morning?

My alarm clock is set for 5:30 AM. I don't know of any successful sales professional who sleeps in. So, just plan on being a part of the "get up early club." It's the only way you are going to be prepared for your day.

For me, work begins at 6 AM with my daily activity sheet. For the next two hours, I am busy preparing all of my activities for the day.

The first page of my activity sheet is dedicated to identifying and listing money-making calls—the people who I believe should be cutting me a check this week. Each and every one must get a call *today!*

My goal is to write a minimum of three deals a week, so for me, that means I must set at least six closes. Your ratio may be different.

Next is my prospecting page. Here, I'm listing the individuals who either have been referred to me or are prospects I have identified. I will typically set ten new opens a week.

You can see the math. Ten opens generate six closes, which produce three sales. Those are my absolute minimums. What about your numbers? How many prospects will you need to get the number of closes you need, to get the number of sales you need every week? This is where the rubber meets the road. If you plug in weak numbers, you will fail. You MUST plug in extreme numbers. Ignore what all of your peers are doing and take a lesson from your industry legends.

My third page is dedicated to GOING BIG. At any given time, I have five to ten ultrahigh net-worth individuals on this list. I will select only one to call TODAY and use some of my early morning time to do some research on the person. You MUST make one big contact each day.

My fourth page is the deal preparation page. I will list every deal that I must prepare for this week. I do this preparation work before 8 AM or after 6 PM only and delegate as much of it as possible to my assistant.

Page five is dedicated to e-mails. I list the correspondence that I must send *today* as well as any responses that I am expecting *today*. I will focus on e-mails before 8 AM, between meetings, and after 6 PM, as well as during any downtime (which hopefully isn't often). Many times, I'm dealing with e-mail at home in the evening.

Page six consists of issues that I need to address with my assistant. I delegate as much as possible to my support staff. I find they are much better at administrative issues than I am. If you are operating without an assistant, and can afford one, you are missing the boat big time. They are worth their weight in gold. I'm fortunate to have the best assistant in the business. She anticipates my needs and over-delivers on running my office.

That's it. Six pages. They take me fifteen to thirty minutes to complete and give me a detailed road map for an extreme day, *before* my day begins. This daily preparation is not optional. Period.

Service Issues

Let's face it. We can't have clients without service-related calls. I get them every day and depend on my administrative staff to handle all but those calls that are sensitive or complex. However, throughout the day, mostly when I'm driving, I will call clients who have a service need to let them know we are working on it. I will also call them once our tasks are completed.

These calls are probably the most effective marketing tool we have. In solving their issues, we become more than a salesperson in their eyes. We are a problem solver. Well-handled service issues create client confidence. Client confidence builds trust. And trust leads to more business and referrals. Next to prospecting, providing excellent service is absolutely the most important thing we can do.

Every time I call a client about the status of a service need, I ask them, "How are you doing? How's business going? Is there anything else I can be doing for you?"

Do you think they are receptive? You bet they are. Who else would a client trust with their next need than the person who has followed through on their commitment to excellent service?

Rules of the Road

On average, I spend at least two hours a day in my car driving to appointments. I hope it is no surprise to you that I use this time to be productive. I make calls, dictate, and think through my next meeting. I always have a Dictaphone in my car. I will dictate tasks from my calls as a reminder. I also use the Dictaphone to note key issues or tasks after each of my meetings. What are you doing in your car? Tapping out a tune on the steering wheel?

Monday

Monday to me is the most important day of the week. An unproductive Monday means an unproductive week. Monday is dedicated to setting appointments—just me, my activity sheet, and the telephone.

The day begins like all of the rest, with setting up my daily activity sheet. At 7:30 AM, I meet with my assistant to discuss administrative issues. And at 8 AM, I begin to call and set as many appointments as I can for each day. I MUST set six closing meetings, ten new prospect meetings, one center-of-influence meeting, and, in between, client review meetings. The only other meeting to which I am open is a vendor meeting at 7:30 AM on Fridays.

Once I have made all of my calls and set my week, if there is any time left, I will prep files for my next day's meetings. I may, on occasion, have an appointment on Monday, but not often.

I will typically stay until about 6:30 PM. The folks I'm trying to reach are busy people. They tend to return their calls late in the day. I believe it makes a great statement that I'm working as hard and long as they are. It sure beats missing their call and playing phone tag!

Tuesday

I begin Tuesdays like every other day; my activity sheet for the day MUST be done. I meet with my assistant at 7:30 AM, prep for going big, and it's off to appointments—returning and taking calls while I'm in the car. I do, however, commit to an hour in the office making calls.

Don't forget, you MUST GO BIG, EVERY DAY. (Remember to warm up with your other calls first!)

As my day winds down, I head back to my office to transfer all of my dictated notes to my client data system. I then straighten up my desk, organize, and reflect on my day. I think about what I did right and what I did wrong. I replay in my mind all of the moments that gave me a RUSH. And then it's off to home.

Wednesday

Hump Day. You now have one extreme day of calling and one full day of appointments behind you. You should have a handful of referrals, new opportunities, and a new mind-set. Wednesday should be very similar to Tuesday—full of new appointments, maybe a BIG MEETING, and new referrals to obtain. I hope you are attacking the day and every meeting with confidence. You must be BOLD in your proposition statement and asking for the deal. Anything less is unacceptable. Once your day is over, reflect. How did you do?

I'm quite sure that after three extreme days, you are going home with a sense of pride and appreciation for your newfound path in sales.

Thursday

You know what to do from 6 AM until 8 AM. How does it feel to kick off your day with a plan and a calendar full of appointments? Remember your commitment to sharpening your opening proposition statement. How are your prospects responding to your new approach?

By now, your colleagues are wondering, "What has gotten into you?" The RUSH is now becoming addictive; you want more and can't wait to do it all over again.

Question: Did you remember to GO BIG? Your day should look, feel, and end just like Wednesday did.

Friday

Ah, it's Friday. It's time to relax, coast a bit, maybe take a half day. WRONG. That's what your buddies do. You're not done yet! You have a 6 AM appointment with your activity sheet. And then for me, I take care of administrative duties and get ready to meet with a vendor.

Vendor meetings are important. I'm always open to exciting new products and services that may benefit my clients. And besides, these meetings give me an excellent opportunity to ask about what other sales reps in my industry are up to—they're a great way to keep an eye on the competition. But the meetings are ALWAYS on my schedule—7:30 AM Friday. No exceptions. (After all, if they are willing to see me then, they must be serious.)

With the vendor meeting done, I head out to my first client or prospecting meeting. I see as many people as I can. I make time to drop into the office, GO BIG, and then go to another meeting.

I like to keep my late Friday afternoons open for prospecting calls. As I have already mentioned, many high net-worth clients call me late Friday. I can't tell you how many times they express appreciation that I'm there. Most of my competitors are out golfing—spending money they don't have and pretending they are someone they are not.

Before I leave for the weekend, I reflect on my day and measure my results. I have meetings already set for next week, usually ten or more referrals to call Monday morning, many closes to set, three to four BIG prospects who owe me a return call, and a LOT of contracts on my desk. What a great way to start off the weekend. I can relax, not stress out about money, spend quality time with my family, and enjoy the fruits of my labor.

And it all began with one extreme day, and then another, and ended with a phenomenal week. My only commitment was to get up one day at a time (early) and focus on my day and tasks. I know … it sounds easy in concept, but can be very hard to stick to every day.

I challenge you to give my week a try. But remember, you only have to commit, plan, and execute it ONE DAY at a time.

One last question for you to ponder: Do you think I found my RUSH in my day and throughout my week?

You bet I did—with every prospecting call and meeting, GOING BIG, asking for and obtaining referrals, delivering the perfect presentation, and taking applications. You can find yours, but it's going to take a change and a new commitment.

What time is it? If it's early enough, you can start TODAY!

Chapter 13: Questions to Consider

- Are you satisfied with your current activities and results?
- What time do you get up each morning?
- Do you create a daily activity list?
- Do you take care of administrative activities before your day begins?
- When do you take care of service issues and account preparation?
- Do you control your schedule?
- Do you have certain activities for each day in the week?
- Would you like to know what an extreme day really feels like?
- Do you know what your sales legends do every day?
- Are you willing to emulate them?
- Can you commit to one extreme day?

How To Survive And Prosper In A Tough Economy

Chapter 14: Get Up or Get Out

Hey, how about that economy?

After being in the business as long as I have, you begin to figure out that nothing lasts forever. Inevitably, a strong economy gives way to tough times. Tough times eventually lead back to a robust economy. It always happens. Plan on it.

Listen, when the economy is in the tank, nobody feels it faster or more severely than a salesperson. Nobody seems to want to buy real estate, banks are not lending, cars are sitting, investment advisors are struggling, and business owners are not moving inventory.

Now we've all heard the classic saying that "when the going gets tough, the tough get going." But when it comes to sales, the not-so-tough also get going—right on out of the profession and in search of safer jobs (if there is such a thing).

So here's my saying about tough times: "Either get up or get out."

Those who stay will only become more in demand once the economy turns around. Those who leave, then come back when times are better, will never enjoy long-term success.

When it comes to a challenging economy, how you respond and position yourself is critical to your success. As an example, I think that many will look back to 2008–2009 as the worst years of their sales career. Not for me. I doubled my income and had the strongest profits of my career—for which I'm grateful.

I sincerely believe that difficult times can create tremendous opportunities for those who seek them out.

How do you prepare? Here are my thoughts.

Challenges

How do you handle financial challenges?

As you know by now, I struggled financially for the first ten years of my career. My first challenge was being new to sales—a problem we all face. The other was being lazy, which produced predictable outcomes: the electricity being shut off, a car being repossessed, and macaroni as my principle entrée—while not fun, it certainly wasn't a reason to give up.

Here's my point: difficult times made me who I am today. I learned from those experiences. I knew that I was on my own, and the only person who could turn things around was me.

While in the middle of an economic meltdown, it's hard to appreciate this, but tough times teach valuable lessons, sharpen selling skills, force outside-of-the-box thinking, and maybe most importantly, help a person appreciate the better times. All of the legends have had their struggles. They believed they would persevere, and they did.

Can you relate?

If you don't believe you can make it through tough times, you're probably right, and you're likely to join the thousands who come and go with the tide. If you believe you can and are willing to do everything it takes to succeed, then you will.

Fear Breeds Opportunity

Fear and greed are prime market motivators. When times are good, everybody wants to jump on board: GREED. But when times are tough, FEAR causes people to jump from an established strategy, potentially leaving you high and dry.

So ask yourself, "Once they jump, where do they land?"

Your answer can put you in front of extraordinary opportunities. For me, I reposition my message and services to address their new needs. If fear is driving their decisions, then safety is my message.

As an example, during challenging times I am absolutely amazed by how many financial advisors just disappear. They stop communicating with their clients at exactly the wrong time. For the most part, clients just want to be kept up-to-date and to know that their advisor is there for them. My point being, that when times are good, sales come easily, and when times are bad, sales can also come easily if you are positioned to serve your prospects' new needs.

Take the time to think through how you can repackage your proposition statement or product/service to meet a prospect's new mind-set. It can be done. Ninety percent of your competition will give up. They cannot or will not take the time to change with the times. Ten percent will figure out that fear is another opportunity.

The math works. There will always be people available to buy your service or product. A given market situation may mean that there are fewer buyers, but inevitably, there will also be fewer salespeople competing for the business. The odds really haven't changed.

I have seen this time and time again. The best real estate, car, pharmaceutical, mortgage, and insurance sales professionals are often busier when times are tough than when they are good. They adapt. They work harder. They believe that buyers still exist.

Work Ethic

This is a no-brainer. If the economy is causing sales to slow, you either create more activity or give up and move on.

I have found that in my industry, bad economic times mean that I need to focus on a larger number of smaller deals to replace the bigger deals that just won't be materializing for the time being. So it's basically work harder, see more deals, earn the same money—which is a much better scenario than blindly doing what has always been done before and going out of business.

Diversification

As mentioned in the chapter "Shooting Rabbits While Elephant Hunting," I believe in a diversified prospecting strategy. If a person only sells high-end homes, gas-guzzling cars, expensive whole-life insurance, jumbo loans, and high-ticket services—tough economic times could be a challenge.

You never want to be held captive by one market. You must seriously consider the concept of a well-diversified product, service, and market.

My diversified strategy doesn't change with the times. I always prospect to several different economic market classes. I just adjust and spend more time with whatever market is hot.

Tough times can create opportunities only for those who adapt. Will you?

Finances

As a financial advisor, I have the opportunity to observe how people plan for bad economic times. Unfortunately, there are very few wealthy sales professionals. Don't get me wrong; there are many salespeople who make a lot of money, but very few know how to create wealth.

Ninety percent of the salespeople I know are showoffs. They believe they must drive expensive cars, live in the best neighborhoods, and wear a lot of bling. All the while, they have no savings, are behind on taxes, and have not been investing in their business.

Quite frankly, the high net-worth salespeople I represent drive modest cars and live in nice neighborhoods. No bling. They are the classic example of the book, *Millionaire Next Door*. To have any chance of surviving tough economic times, people MUST have substantial savings and their debt under control.

Besides, high net-worth prospects despise salespeople who project themselves to be someone they are not. It's a lie in their eyes, and they find it very hard to trust someone who is not true to themselves. Big prospects also assume that flashy salespeople are charging too much to support their lavish lifestyle. I have always been a believer in modesty. Big prospects respect modesty and live by the same standards.

In order to survive economic challenges, you must prepare for them when times are good. When you are making significant money, pay down debt and save. Unfortunately, many people just ratchet up their lifestyle a few notches.

Do not let tough times catch you by surprise. They will happen. Be prepared to weather the storm. In short, get your financial act together.

Peers

When times are tough, we all feel the pain and at times can get down. To me, there is nothing more depressing than being surrounded by a bunch of negative, whiny salespeople.

I have surrounded myself with very optimistic and successful sales professionals from various industries. They have my back. They encourage me when I'm down, motivate me when I want to coast, and get in my face when I need it. My commitment is to do the same for them. These relationships have been crucial to my growth and success.

Who do you associate with?

As it turns out, successful salespeople from outside your industry are also great sources of new business. The professionals in my group are working just as hard as I am. Together, we introduce each other to our clients. My successful peers are also great resources for new ideas and concepts. We share our marketing strategies, groups we belong to, and market insights.

As I have already stated, the truly successful sales professionals I know give more than they take. They care about you, your family, and your success. Do you have someone in your business life who you respect, admire, and care about? If not, find one. They may make the difference when times are tough.

These are the concepts I live by in good times and bad. It is imperative that you evaluate your game plan and mind-set if you find yourself in a difficult spot. The strong will survive the tough times and thrive in good. Legends of the past and present know and understand these concepts. They have worked for them. They have worked for me. I hope that is enough evidence to prove that they can work for you too.

Chapter 14: Questions to Consider

- Do bad economic times challenge you?
- Have you lost your confidence?
- Do you need inspiration?
- Do you know that the 10 percenters, in good times and bad, will always perform at extreme levels?
- Do you want to know how and why?
- How do you handle financial challenges?
- Do you believe people are driven by fear and greed?
- Are your prospecting efforts diversified?
- Do you have your financial house in order?
- Do you hang out with negative salespeople?
- Do you know without a doubt you will make it in this business?

_____

_____

_____

_____

_____

_____

_____

_____

_____

_____

_____

_____

_____

_____

_____

_____

_____

Your Future As A Master Sales Professional

Chapter 15: A Legend is Born

Okay, I have to ask. Did you feel anything?

I mean, you've read fourteen chapters now. Did you experience any anger? A little frustration? Maybe some hope or desire? Enthusiasm? Pride? Maybe even a RUSH or two?

Well, I hope so! Your sales game depends on it. After all, emotions drive our behavior. They give us our edge. They put us in the top 10 percent, but only if we understand how to control and use them to our advantage—*every day.*

Your emotions are a gift. Your mission is to use this gift, emulate the successes of others, and become the sales professional you aspire to be.

I also hope that you have come to realize that this is *not* rocket science. There are no secret formulas for success—just hard work. *RUSH* has simply communicated the fundamentals as practiced *every day* by the true legends of our industry. My goal has been to bring these concepts forward and show you how to apply them to today's challenges.

While your industry may be very different than mine, the fundamentals of sales still apply. They apply to all industries. Your job is to customize these fundamental truths and put them into action.

In doing so, remember you must:

- First, find your RUSH and then,

- Focus on implementing that RUSH strategy *one day* at a time.

The adrenaline we seek and crave is there for those who challenge themselves *every day*. It's readily available by doing the very things that most people will not do.

I'm very proud of our industry and thankful for how I was wired. It is very gratifying to do something I love while bringing so much value to the people I meet.

Sales organizations often reward their top performers by sending them on all-expense-paid trips to places all over the world. I have been fortunate to attend many of these events and have had the opportunity to get to know sales greats personally—many of them making seven-figure incomes on a consistent basis. I have always been amazed by what I learn.

They are very gracious, humble, and appreciative. They appear to be happily married and very committed to their families. They're modest and sincere. Many are well into their sixties, but never discuss retirement. They are full of life and love going to work. They are fulfilled and content with their lives.

I'm down for that any day! How about you? Look to the legends and top sales performers in your industry; do they stand for what you want in life? If yes, study everything they do and emulate them as much as possible.

You have a tremendous opportunity to control your destiny, income, and future. Remember, 90 percent of those who enter the sales industry fail. You're a part of the 10 percent who made it. Your next challenge is to be in the top 10 percent of that group. Do the math. That would make you a "1 percenter." A very rare breed indeed!

So where are you in your professional development? New to the business? Your office isn't coming through with quality training? You're surrounded by mediocrity? You're trying to figure out a game plan for a successful career? I respect your enthusiasm to learn and achieve and can very much relate to it. I hope you found everything you were looking for in *RUSH*. Please come back again and again to sharpen your focus and recommit your energies.

Have you been in the sales industry for a while? Frustrated? Confused? Broke? Yep, I've been there—many times. No direction, stuck in a rut, and wasting time on ineffective strategies. And let's face it, the confidence is shot. Fortunately, there is a way out. The fundamentals that are taught in *RUSH* can be implemented TODAY. It only takes a renewed commitment to just one extreme day of intense work—just you, the phone, and your daily activity sheet.

You can do it. It's not complicated. Follow the proven path and measure your results. Don't let anyone get in your way. Find a legend. Read a book written by one of your industry's greats. Enroll in an educational program. Get busy. There are no more excuses!

And then again, maybe you are already well on your way to becoming a legend. You know and practice the fundamental truths. I hope you found *RUSH* confirming. Your job is to spread the message. Share this book and your time helping others. They need you. I have found the more I help others, the more accountable I become. The more I share my knowledge, the more I commit to my beliefs. You and I have an obligation to lead. Our industry needs more professionals stepping up. New sales reps need our wisdom and guidance. Our industry needs to be cleaned up and brought back to the respect it deserves. I would appreciate your help and hope to meet you someday.

I know that you can go to any bookstore or Web site to read about sales. New books are being written every day by people who have never sold anything in their life. They can't even sell their own book. They hire a firm to do that. I purposely never considered hiring a firm to sell *RUSH*. I wanted to be responsible for my own sales, practice what I preach. I believe it would be hypocritical to hire someone else to do the very thing I know best.

I hope you found *RUSH* to be authentic, refreshing, and honest. I live the life of a salesman *every day*. I have shared with you my victories and defeats. I know without a doubt my future is secure. I strive, one day at a time, to someday be referred to as a legend. Not yet, but some day very soon.

I wish you the very best in your sales career. There is much more to come from me and others who are present-day sales masters. Please read my final chapter, "4Myrush.com." I have very exciting news.

While it's the end of this book, it's a new beginning for you.

Chapter 15: Questions to Consider

- Did you feel something that maybe you haven't in a long time while reading *RUSH*?
- Do you believe you were made to be in sales?
- Do you understand that our legends of the past have left you and me the gift of how to sell at an extreme level?
- Do you feel reborn and prepared for a new mind-set?
- Do you understand that nothing is new to the fundamentals of sales?
- Are you considering studying the legends of your past and stars of our present?
- Do you know that very few people can do what you can do?
- Do you understand that very few people have the opportunity you have?
- Are you ready to achieve greatness and be the person you have always dreamed of being?
- Last question: Will you do it?

_____

_____

_____

_____

_____

_____

_____

_____

_____

_____

_____

_____

_____

_____

_____

_____

_____

A Resource For The Salesperson Who Desires Extreme Results

Chapter 16: 4myrush.com

There's sales. And then there's extreme sales.

Just about everyone thinks they're an expert in sales—whether they have ever sold anything or not. A quick trip to the bookstore or a visit to Amazon.com is proof of that!

I hope this doesn't come as a surprise, but if you don't know by now, I'm addicted to learning everything I can from sales legends and today's top sales professionals. If you share this passion with me, then you probably share my frustration in not having a resource that offers extreme sales professionals the tools we need.

Done!

I'm proud to announce 4myrush.com.

4myrush.com is a Web site for sales professionals seeking the very best sales tools available—produced by sales professionals for sales professionals, all with proven results.

Depending on when you are reading this, the site may be just about ready to launch or fully up and running. In any event, it is very interactive and designed for continually bringing you new concepts and strategies.

Here's a look at what you will find:

STUDY GUIDES that further explore the basic concepts laid out in *RUSH*, including:

- Death by a Thousand Distractions

- Seek Out Your Industry Legends
- Shooting Rabbits While Elephant Hunting
- Go Big
- Get Up or Get Out

SALES IDEAS for addressing *today's* market challenges. With sales professionals contributing ideas from a wide range of industries, we can adapt the strategies of others to our own unique situations. We will value your input.

BOOK REVIEWS to ensure you are making the best use of your reading time. Please nominate books you have found to be excellent. I will share books that I believe will be of value. Some of the most profound books may not even be about sales, yet carry a very strong message for us.

ELECTRONIC NEWSLETTER focusing on sales, strategies, concepts, and relevant news. Your ideas and interests will again be of great importance as we delve into issues such as:

- Obtaining referrals
- Closing deals
- Prospecting
- Marketing
- Measuring results
- Technology tools

SALES JOB-RELATED INFORMATION will be posted for those looking for new opportunities.

YOUR FEEDBACK AND INPUT is the most important component of the whole site. We want to hear from you. Your feedback and input is vital to the site's success. We all can learn from one another and become better for it. I look forward to communicating with you.

We are working hard to pull it all together and will launch different tools as they become available. I also have many other books and ideas running through my head. We would love to hear your ideas as well.

Please e-mail me (bob@4myrush.com) your thoughts on the launch of this site, and I will let you know when we go live at 4myrush. com.

See you soon.

Bob